PHOTO CREDITS

Color illustrations by Bert Dodson and Eulala Conner.

Editorial Development Lois Eskin, Alice Trimmer, June Wolfberg
Editorial Processing Margaret M. Byrne, Regina Chilcoat, Holly L. Massey
Art and Production Fred C. Pusterla, Robin Swenson, Vivian Fenster, Paula Darmofal, Barbara Orzech, Russell Dian, Anita Dickhuth, Ellen Lokiec
Product Manager J. Edward Johnson
Advisory Board James Boyd, William G. Jones, David Joy, Sheila Nettles
Consultants Sheila Nettles, Ruth Spies
Researchers Eileen Kelly, Pamela Floch, Gerard LaVan

CONTENTS

MUSIC TO EXPLORE

The First Quarter

THE MUSIC BOOK

Eunice Boardman
Professor of Music Education
University of Wisconsin
Madison, Wisconsin

Barbara Andress
Professor of Music Education
Arizona State University
Tempe, Arizona

Special Consultants

Beth Landis
Former Director of Music Education
City Schools
Riverside, California

Betty Welsbacher
Director of Special Music Education
Wichita State University
Wichita, Kansas

Consultants

Martha Mahoney
Elementary Music Department Head
Elementary Schools
Milford, Connecticut

Donald Regier
Supervisor of Vocal Music
Secondary Schools
Baltimore County, Maryland

Keith Thompson
Associate Professor, Music Education
Pennsylvania State University
University Park, Pennsylvania

Nelmatilda Woodard
Director, Bureau of Music Education
Board of Education
City of Chicago

Holt, Rinehart and Winston, Publishers
New York, Toronto, London, Sydney

ISBN: 0-03-042201-9
123456 071 98765432

ACKNOWLEDGMENTS

Grateful acknowledgment is given to the following authors and publishers:

American Ethical Union for "Brethren in Peace Together." Copyright © 1955: The American Ethical Union Library Catalog number 54:11625. Used by permission.

Atheneum Publishers, Inc., for "The Snake" from *Sweetly Sings The Donkey: Animal Rounds for Children to Sing or Play on Recorders*, selected by John Langstaff (A Margaret K. McElderry Book). Text copyright © 1976 by John Langstaff. Used by permission.

BJE Choral Series, Jewish Education Committee for "Sabbath Queen." Used by permission.

Chappell Music Company for "A Horse Named Bill," from *Jerry Silverman's Folk Song Encyclopedia*; for "The Lonely Goatherd" from *The Sound of Music* by Richard Rodgers and Oscar Hammerstein. Copyright © 1959 by Richard Rodgers and Oscar Hammerstein II and Williamson Music, Inc. All Rights Reserved. Used by permission of Chappell & Co. Inc., on behalf of Williamson Music, Inc.

Cherry Lane Music Co. for "Sunshine on My Shoulders" by John Denver, Dick Kniss, and Mike Taylor.

George M. Cohan Publishing Company for "Yankee Doodle Boy" by George M. Cohan. Copyright by George M. Cohan Publishing Company. Used by permission.

Christopher Davis Ltd. for melody to "Migildi Magildi" from *Welsh Songs* by J. Lloyd Williams and L. D. Jones. Used by permission.

Mrs. Ira Eisenstein for original words to the Hasidic tune "Harvest." Used by permission.

Fall River Music Inc. for *Guantanamera* (Guajiro Guantanamero). Original lyrics and music by Jose Fernandez Dias (Joseito Fernandez). Music adaptation by Pete Seeger. Lyric adaptation by Hector Angulo, based on a poem by Jose Marti. Copyright © 1963, 1965 by Fall River Music, Inc. All rights reserved. Used by permission.

Frank Music Corp. for "The Inch Worm" by Frank Loesser.

Ginn & Company for words and melody line of "Ode to a Washerwoman—Rondo on Eight Familiar Melodies" from *More Partner Songs* by Frederick Beckman. Arrangement by Frederick Beckman. Used by permission.

Girl Scouts for "Whippoorwill Round" from *Ditty Bag* compiled by Janet Tobitt. Used by permission.

Gulf Music Company for arrangement to "Abalone" and for words to "Sweet Potatoes" and "Farewell, My Own True Love" by William S. Haynie. Copyright © 1966 by Gulf Music Company. Used by permission.

Hansen Publications for "La Cucaracha" from *1001 Folk Tunes*. Copyright © 1976 by Shattinger International Music Co. Used by permission.

Harcourt Brace Jovanovich, Inc., for "The Farmer Is The Man" from *The American Songbook* by Carl Sandburg. Used by permission.

Harwin Music Company for "Ac-cent-tchu-ate the Positive" lyrics by Johnny Mercer, music by Harold Arlen. Copyright 1944 by Harwin Music Company, renewed © 1972 by Harwin Music Company. Used by permission.

Holt, Rinehart and Winston, Publishers, for the poem "Dust of Snow" from *You Come Too* by Robert Frost. Copyright 1928 by Holt, Rinehart and Winston, Publishers. Copyright 1951 by Robert Frost. Used by permission.

Macmillan Publishing Co. Inc. for "In the Pines" from *The Blue Grass Songbook* edited by Dennis Cyporyn. Copyright © 1972 Macmillan/Collier Books. Used by permission.

Edward B. Marks Corporation for "Lift Every Voice and Sing" by J. Rosamond Johnson and James Weldon Johnson. Copyright 1921 and later renewed by Edward B. Marks Corporation. Used by permission.

Northern Music Company for "Magic Penny" by Malvina Reynolds. Copyright © 1955, © 1958 by Northern Music Company, New York, N.Y. All rights reserved. Used by permission.

Oxford University Press for the English words by Jack Dobbs to "Migildi Magildi" from *The Oxford School Music Book*. Copyright Oxford University Press, London. Used by permission.

Theodore Presser Company, sole representative in the United States for Durand et Cie, for "Voiles" from *Book 1 of Preludes for Piano* by Claude Debussy. Copyright 1910 by Durand et Cie. For "Putnam's Camp" from *Three Places in New England* by Charles Ives. Copyright 1935 by Mercury Music Corporation. Used by permission.

The Richmond Organization—TRO—for "So Long" (It's Been Good To Know Yuh), "This Land Is Your Land," "If I Had A Hammer," "Go Down The Wishin' Road," "Food, Glorious Food," "Where Is Love?" "Consider Yourself," "I'd Do Anything," and "Who Will Buy?" Used by permission.

AMERICA, AMERICA

Traditional

Sing as a round.

Add an accompaniment.

A - mer - i - ca, A - mer - i - ca!

Shall I tell you how we ___ feel?

You have giv - en us your ___ beau - ty

We sing to you. ___

BASS XYLOPHONE:

PLEDGE OF ALLEGIANCE TO THE FLAG

Musical Setting by Irving Caesar

I pledge al - le - giance, pledge al - le - giance, Pledge al -

le - giance to the flag, To the flag of the U -

nit - ed States of A - mer - i - ca, A - mer - i - ca, And

to the Re - pub - lic for which it stands!

Chorus

One Na - tion un - der God, One Na - tion un - der

God, In - di - vis - i - ble with lib - er - ty and

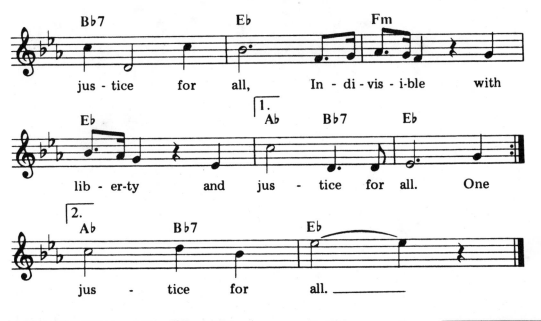

jus - tice for all, In - di - vis - i-ble with
lib - er-ty and jus - tice for all. One
jus - tice for all. _____

U.S. Presidents

1. **All:** Chant the refrain.
2. **First Solo:** Chant verse 1. **All:** Chant verse 1 and the refrain.
3. **Second Solo:** Chant verse 2. **All:** Chant verse 2, verse 1, and the refrain.
4. Continue this pattern, naming all of the Presidents.

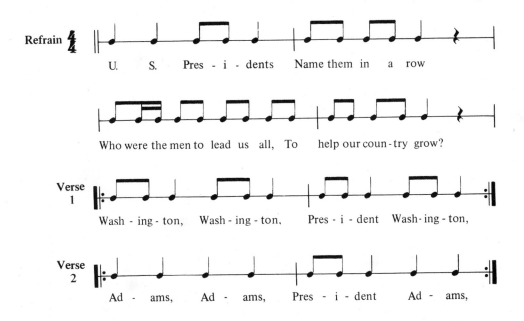

Refrain

U. S. Pres - i - dents Name them in a row

Who were the men to lead us all, To help our coun - try grow?

Verse 1

Wash - ing - ton, Wash - ing - ton, Pres - i - dent Wash - ing - ton,

Verse 2

Ad - ams, Ad - ams, Pres - i - dent Ad - ams,

FIFTY, NIFTY UNITED STATES

Words and Music by Ray Charles

Fif - ty, Nif - ty, U - ni - ted States, From thir-teen o-rig-i-nal col - o-nies, Fif - ty, nif - ty stars in the flag That bil-lows so beau-tif - 'ly in— the breeze, Each in - di - vi-du-al state Con- tri-butes a qual-i-ty that is great Each in - di-

4

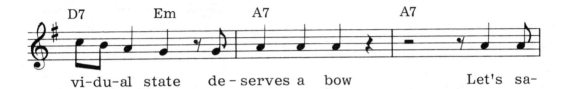

vi-du-al state de-serves a bow Let's sa-

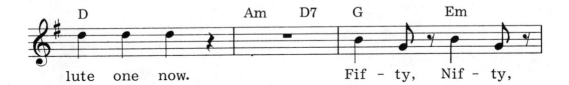

lute one now. Fif — ty, Nif — ty,

U — ni — ted States From thir — teen o-rig-i — nal

col — o-nies, Shout 'em, scout 'em, tell all a-bout 'em

One by one till we've had_ our say For ev-'ry state

in the U. S. A._____

HOE-DOWN
from *Rodeo*

by Aaron Copland

CALL CHART

CALL 1	**Introduction**	"Get ready for a wild square dance!" The strings tune up. The piano, strings, and wood block set the rhythms for dancing.

2	**A**	The square dance begins with fiddle tunes.
		The xylophone and other instruments
		    help to liven up the dance.
		The section ends with strings, brass, and winds, playing
		
		       mf $\diagup\!\!\!\!\diagdown$ *p*

3	**B** The trumpet begins a new, syncopated melody. 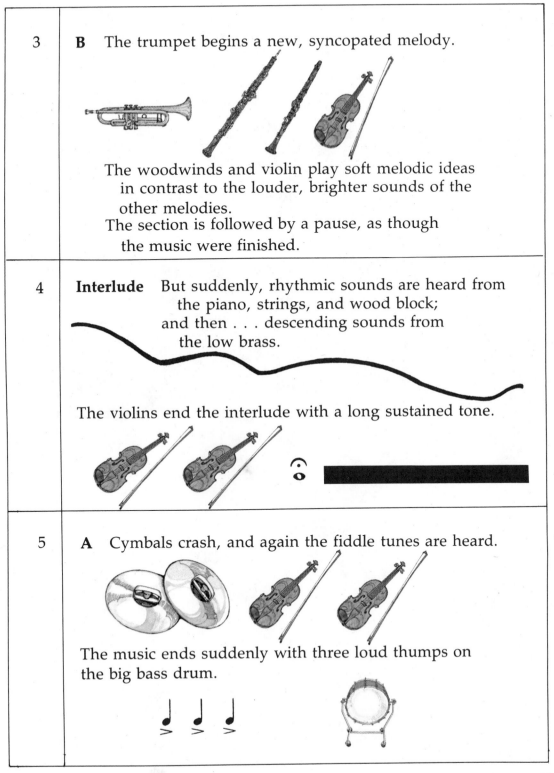 The woodwinds and violin play soft melodic ideas in contrast to the louder, brighter sounds of the other melodies. The section is followed by a pause, as though the music were finished.
4	**Interlude** But suddenly, rhythmic sounds are heard from the piano, strings, and wood block; and then . . . descending sounds from the low brass. The violins end the interlude with a long sustained tone.
5	**A** Cymbals crash, and again the fiddle tunes are heard. The music ends suddenly with three loud thumps on the big bass drum.

SONGS FOR REMEMBERING

Can you remember these songs?
Sing them as though you were hearing them on the radio.
Choose one person to turn the radio on to begin the music.
When the radio is turned off, you can no longer hear the music.
Does the song continue?
When the radio is turned on again, what part
of the song should you sing?

HAPPINESS RUNS IN A CIRCULAR MOTION ...

HEY! HO! ANYBODY HOME ...

OH, I WENT DOWN SOUTH FOR TO SEE MY GAL SINGING .....

THE OLD GREY MARE, ...

OH, BEAUTIFUL FOR .....

≡ A Melody to Remember ≡

How well can you recall the melody of a new song?
Follow the words as you listen to the recording.
Learn the melody by listening.

≡≡ ACCENTUATE THE POSITIVE ≡≡

Words by Johnny Mercer   Music by Harold Arlen

You've got to ACCENTUATE THE POSITIVE,
Eliminate the negative,
Latch on to the affirmative,
Don't mess with Mister In–between.

You've got to spread joy up to the maximum,
Bring gloom down to the minimum,
Have faith or pandemonium
'Li'ble to walk upon the scene.

To illustrate . . . my last remark
Jonah in the whale, Noah in the Ark,
What did they do just when everything look so dark?

"Man," they said,
"We better ACCENTUATE THE POSITIVE,
Eliminate the negative,
Latch on to the affirmative,
Don't mess with Mister In–between."
No! Don't mess with Mister In–between.

ODE TO A WASHERWOMAN

Traditional Folk Song
Arranged by Fred Bockman

Oh, dear, what can the mat - ter be?

Oh, dear, what can the mat - ter be?

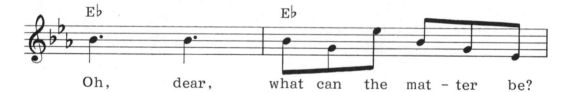

Oh, dear, what can the mat - ter be?

My maid has gone to the fair. _____

Choose your part - ner, skip to my Lou,

Choose your part - ner, skip to my Lou,

Choose your part - ner skip to my Lou,

Skip to my Lou, my dar - ling.

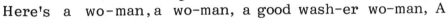

Here's a wo-man, a wo-man, a good wash-er wo-man, A

wo-man, a wo-man, a good wash-er wo-man, A

wo-man, a wo-man, a good wash-er wo-man, She

dan - ces and sings as she wash - es the clothes.

Sing these songs. Create an ABA form.
How many songs will you use?
Create a rondo form.
How many songs will you use?

ACCOMPANY YOUR SONGS

OH DEAR, WHAT CAN THE MATTER BE?

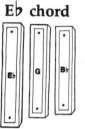

THE GOOD WASHERWOMAN

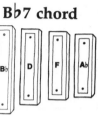

SKIP TO MY LOU

Use these bells.

Eb chord   Bb7 chord   Ab chord

Plan an accompaniment for each song.
Use the **Eb**, **Ab**, and **Bb7** chords.
Sing and accompany all three songs at the same time.
Why is it possible to have a good sound when singing all three
    songs at the same time?

Ice Is Nice

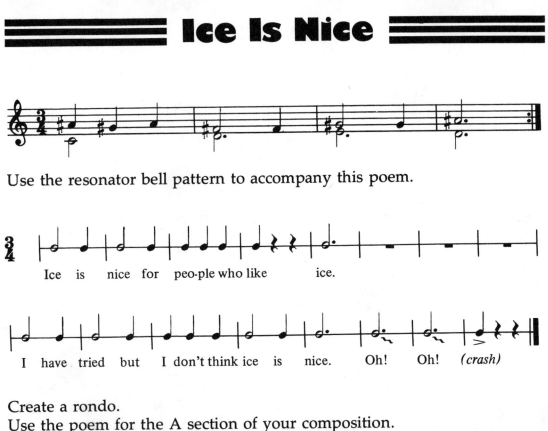

Use the resonator bell pattern to accompany this poem.

Ice   is   nice   for   peo-ple who like   ice.

I   have   tried   but   I   don't think ice   is   nice.   Oh!   Oh!   *(crash)*

Create a rondo.
Use the poem for the A section of your composition.
Continue the bell accompaniment throughout the entire composition.
Create B, C, and D sections for the rondo.
Use these pitches: C, D, E, F♯, G♯, A♯.

WALTZ ON THE ICE
from *Winter Holiday*

by Sergei Prokofiev

Listen to this music. How is it similar to the composition you
have just performed? How is it different?

meter   melody
                form   rhythmic patterns
    tonality
                    dynamics
        articulation   tempo

DOBBIN, DOBBIN

Dutch Tune

Wood block:

Sing the verse and refrain while someone taps the shortest sound.

1. Dob-bin, Dob-bin on your way, We've been to-geth-er For
2. Dob-bin, Dob-bin don't you stop, Just let your feet go

man - y a day, So let your tail go swish as the
clip - pe - ty clop and let your tail go swish as the

wheels go 'round, Gid-dy-ap! We're home-ward bound.
wheels go 'round, Gid-dy-ap! We're home-ward bound.

14

I like to take a horse and bug-gy

When I go trav-'ling to the town.

I like to hear old Dob-bin's clip-clop.

I like to feel the wheels go 'round. ____

Is it possible to sing this music as a partner song?
Look at the music. What will help you decide?

SWINGING ALONG

Scout Song

Here is another partner song.
There are two melodies. The first is written below the second.
Follow the first melody with your fingertips as you listen.
Follow the second melody.
What clue in the **score** tells you to sing the two melodies at the same time?

16

Swing-ing a-long, swing-ing a-long the o-pen road, ___

long, swing a-long, swing a-long the o-pen road, ___

All in the fall of the year.

TEARIN', TARIN', TAPPIN' TOE

How well can you **hear, remember,** and **repeat** a rhythm pattern?
Divide the class into two groups and play a rhythm game.

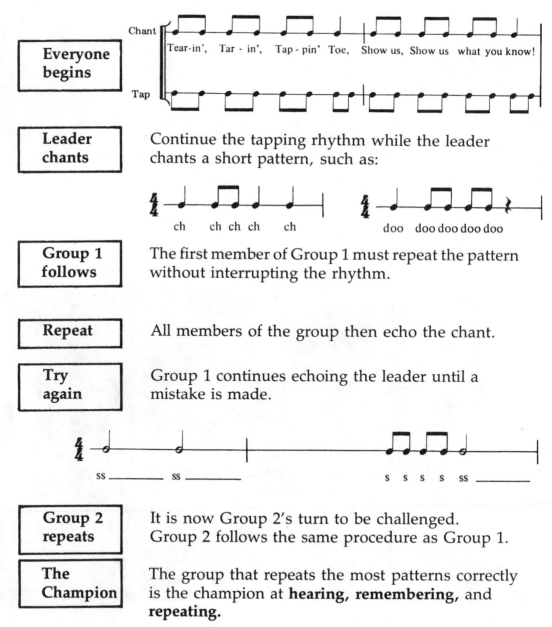

Everyone begins	
Leader chants	Continue the tapping rhythm while the leader chants a short pattern, such as:
Group 1 follows	The first member of Group 1 must repeat the pattern without interrupting the rhythm.
Repeat	All members of the group then echo the chant.
Try again	Group 1 continues echoing the leader until a mistake is made.
Group 2 repeats	It is now Group 2's turn to be challenged. Group 2 follows the same procedure as Group 1.
The Champion	The group that repeats the most patterns correctly is the champion at **hearing, remembering,** and **repeating.**

MY AUNT CAME BACK

How many things can you do at the same time?
Can you chant rhythmically while performing motions?

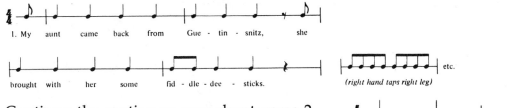

1. My aunt came back from Gue - tin - snitz, she
brought with her some fid - dle - dee - sticks.

(right hand taps right leg)

Continue the motion as you chant verse 2.

2. My aunt came back from Kalamazoo,
   She brought with her some walkin' shoes.

(left-right walking feet)

3. My aunt came back from old Sioux Falls,
   She brought with her some basketballs.

(left hand pats left hip)

4. My aunt came back from old Holmstock,
   She brought with her a crazy clock.

(tongue click)

Add the movement of each new stanza to the previous movements.
How well can you do all four motions at the same time?

Which motion uses the shortest sounds?
Which motion is twice as long as the shortest sound?

Add the sounds of instruments to the chants.
Which instrument will you choose to play:
"fiddle-dee-sticks"? "walkin' shoes"?
"basketballs"? "crazy clock"?

BLACK-EYED SUSIE

Traditional

What do you notice about the rhythm of the melody?

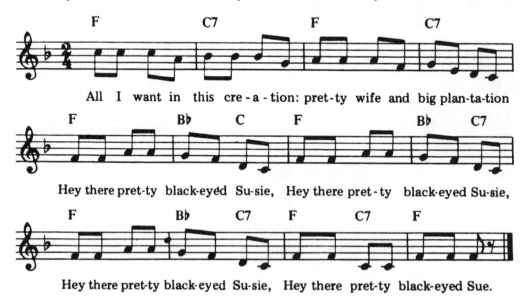

All I want in this cre-a-tion: pret-ty wife and big plan-ta-tion

Hey there pret-ty black-eyed Su-sie, Hey there pret-ty black-eyed Su-sie,

Hey there pret-ty black-eyed Su-sie, Hey there pret-ty black-eyed Sue.

Here is the rhythm of "Black-Eyed Susie" shown in relation to the shortest sound.

Keep tapping the shortest sound as you chant verse 2.
When does the rhythm of the melody change?

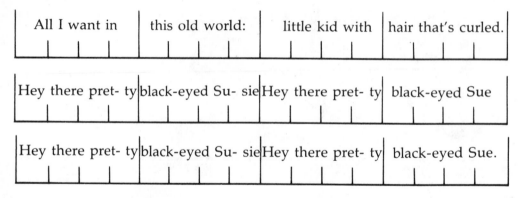

| All I want in | this old world: | little kid with | hair that's curled. |

| Hey there pret- ty | black-eyed Su- sie | Hey there pret- ty | black-eyed Sue |

| Hey there pret- ty | black-eyed Su- sie | Hey there pret- ty | black-eyed Sue. |

Can you write the rhythm of the melody for this verse in notes?
What new note will you have to use?

Chant the words of verse 3 while tapping the shortest sound.
When do you need to change the rhythm?

Verse 3: All I want on earth; happiness and mirth.
Hey! Black-eyed Susie! Hey! Sue!
Hey! Black-eyed Susie! Hey! Sue!

Can you write the rhythm of this verse with notes?
Which note will you need to add?

Divide into three groups.
Try singing all three verses at the same time.
When do you sing the same rhythm?
When is the rhythm different?
Discuss the relationship of the three notes to each other.

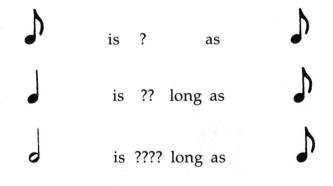

WANDERIN'

American Folk Song

Tap these short sounds
and chant the words.

I've been work-in' in the cit - y I've been work-in' on the farm,

But all I've got to show for it is mus-cle in my arm,

And it looks like I'm nev-er gon-na cease

my wan der - in'.

Discuss the **relationship** of the sounds in the chant to the
short sounds you tapped.
When is the rhythm of the words the **same** as the short
tapping sounds?
On which words is the rhythm **twice as long?**
three times as long?
four times as long?
six times as long?

Now that you know the rhythm, learn the melody.
Can some people add the harmony part?

C   G

1. I've been work-in' in the cit - y, I've been work-in' on the farm,
2. Oh, the blue sky up a - bove me, and the green grass on the ground;

F   Dm   C   Dm

But all I've got to show for it is mus - cle in my arm,
Been look - in' round for man - y things that I have nev - er found,

C   Am   Dm   Dm   G7   C

And it looks like I'm nev- er gon - na cease my wan - der - in'.

DOWN IN THE VALLEY

Arranged by Kurt Miller

Kentucky Folk Song

Down in the val - ly   the val - ley so low _____

1. Down in the val - ley, the val - ley so low, ___ Hang your head
2. Ros - es love sun - shine, __ vio - lets love dew, ___ An - gels in
3. Writ - ing a let - ter con - tain - ing three lines, ___ Ask - ing a

(Melody)

o - ver, hear the wind blow. __ Hear the wind blow, dear, hear the wind
heav - en know I love you, ___ Know I love you, dear, know I love
ques - tion, will you be mine? __ Will you be mine, dear, will you be

blow, __ Hang your head o - ver, hear the wind blow. __
you, __ An - gels in heav - en know I love you. __
mine? __ Ask - ing a ques - tion, will you be mine? __

Keelmen Heaving in Coals by Moonlight, Joseph Mallord William Turner.
National Gallery of Art, Washington, D.C. Widener Collection.

ADAGIO FOR PERCUSSION

Play "Adagio for Percussion."

Part 1: Use high-pitched metal instruments
to play long, ringing sounds.

Part 2: Play short sounds on wood instruments.
Use low, middle, and high pitches.

Part 3: Use low-pitched metal instruments
to play long, ringing sounds.

Follow the expressive markings as you perform.

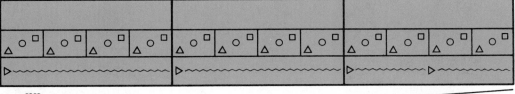

Listen to the music on the next page.
Can you hear anything that is similar to what you just performed?

MOONLIGHT SONATA
First Movement: *Adagio*

by Ludwig van Beethoven

Listen to this music as it is performed on the piano.
Notice the short sounds in the accompaniment that are heard throughout the composition.

The melody is made up mostly of sustained, *legato* sounds.
After listening to the performance, can you decide what these words and symbols mean?

adagio sostenuto   *pp*   *p*   *mf*   <

Listen to another performance of this composition. This time
it is played by full orchestra.
Why do you hear the different parts more distinctly?

DARK ECHO

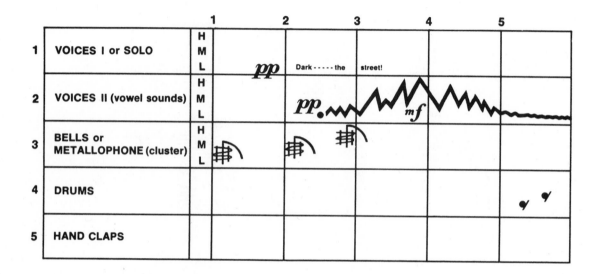

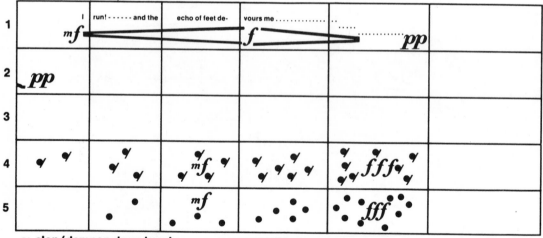

⚫ slap/dampen drum head

Can you:
- perform an *ostinato*?
- arrange partner songs?
- identify rondo form?

- hear rhythms in relation to the shortest unit of sound?
- improvise an interlude?

═ ═ **MORNING COMES EARLY** ═ ═

Words Adapted

Slovak Folk Song

1. Morn - ing comes ear - ly, the dew so bright.
2. Lis - ten, my com - rade: when work seems long,

Come with me, lad - die, in day's first light.
Light - en each mo - ment with mer - ry song.

Dawn o - ver - takes me, morn - ing a - wakes me,
Wel - come to - mor - row, wait not for sor - row,

To the green mead - ows the herd I lead.
Mu - sic and laugh - ter are all we need!

Improvise your interlude over this harmonic accompaniment.

$\frac{2}{4}$ | C | C | G7 | C :‖

LIFT EVERY VOICE AND SING

Words by James Weldon Johnson

Music by J. Rosamond Johnson

Lift ev - ery voice and sing Till earth and heav - en ring,

Ring with the har - mo - nies of lib - er - ty;

Let our re - joic - ing rise High as the list - 'ning — skies,

Let it re - sound loud as the roll - ing sea.

Sing a song full of the faith that the dark past has taught us,

Sing a song full of the hope that the pres - ent has brought us.

Fac-ing the ris - ing sun Of our new day be - gun,
Let us march on till vic-to-ry ___ is won. ___

The musical terms in the score tell you how to perform the music.
Turn to page 35 to discover the meaning of each term.

SETTING THE TEMPO FOR MUSIC

Say "one thousand and one more" over and over.
Make each word or syllable the same length.

one thou - sand   and   one   more,   one   thou - sand   and   one   more,   one   thou - . . .

Continue the pattern as shown below. This time clap on the boxed-in syllables or words.

Repeat several times; then "think" the words while continuing to clap. Each clap will equal the length of one **beat** in the **tempo** named.

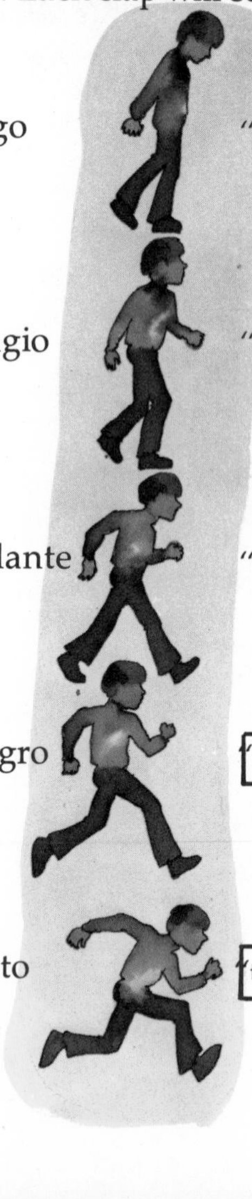

Largo   "one $\boxed{thou}$- sand   and   one   more,   one $\boxed{thou}$- sand   and   one

Adagio   "one $\boxed{thou}$- sand   one,   one $\boxed{thou}$- sand   one"

Andante   "one $\boxed{thou}$- sand,   one $\boxed{thou}$- sand"

Allegro   "$\boxed{thou}$- sand, $\boxed{thou}$- sand"

Presto   "$\boxed{thou}$-$\boxed{sand}$ $\boxed{thou}$-$\boxed{sand}$"

FOLLOW THE SCORE

You will often find terms written in **Italian** in your music.
These terms tell you what expression to use in performance.
Can you decide what each term means by looking at the
visual description?

maestoso

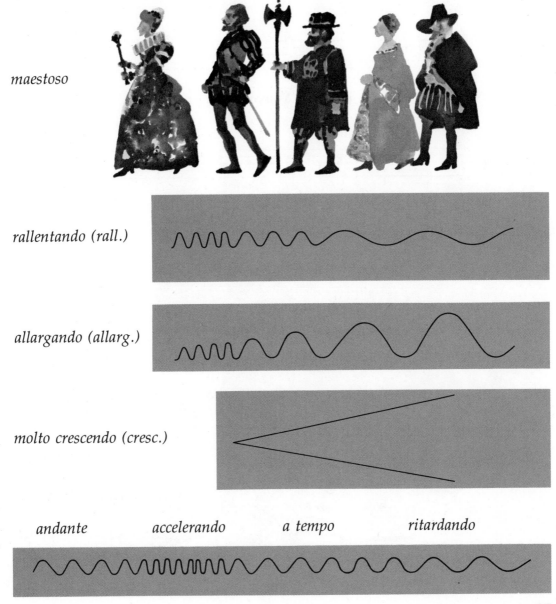

rallentando (rall.)

allargando (allarg.)

molto crescendo (cresc.)

andante   *accelerando*   *a tempo*   *ritardando*

UP WITH PEOPLE

Words and Music
by Paul and Ralph Colwell

How will this piece sound when sung
Largo?　　*Andante?*　　*Allegro?*　　*Presto?*

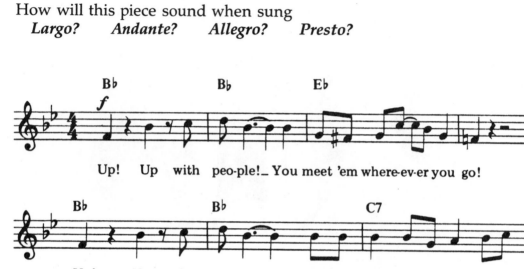

Up!　Up　with　peo-ple!＿ You meet 'em where-ev-er you go!

Up!　Up　with　peo-ple!＿ They're the best kind of folks we know.

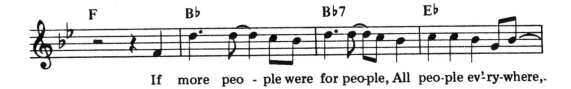

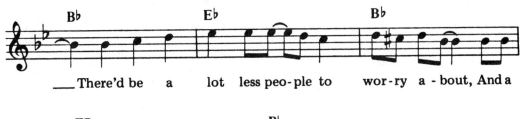

If more peo-ple were for peo-ple, All peo-ple ev'-ry-where,.

___There'd be a lot less peo-ple to wor-ry a-bout, And a

lot more peo-ple who care!

At which tempo is this song most expressive?

≡ TIME, SILENCE, SOUND ≡

Divide into four groups. Choose a conductor for each group.

Conductor of Group 1: Establish an *andante* tempo.
Give the signal for all to begin.

Group members:
- Perform your assigned sound for four beats.
- Count silently for the number of beats given in the score for your group.
- Repeat your assigned sound for four beats.
- Count silently for one beat less than before.
- Continue sounds and silences until you reach zero.
- Continue repeating your sound over and over.

Group 1 (count silently)

♩ ♩ ♩ ♩
SH SH SH SH

1 2 3 4 5 6 7 8 9 10 11 12 13 14 15

♩ ♩ ♩ ♩
SH SH SH SH

1 2 3 4 5 6 7 8 9 10 11 12 13 14

♩ ♩ ♩ ♩
SH SH SH SH

1 2 3 4 5 6 7 8 9 10 11 12 13

(and so on until zero is reached)

Group 2

R r r r r r r r

■ ■ ■ ■   1 2 3 4 5 6 7 8

Group 3

R r r r r r r r

■ ■ ■ ■   1 2 3 4 5 6 7 8 9 10 11

Group 4

3 · 3 · 3 · 3

rag-ged-y rag-ged-y rag-ged-y rag-ged-y   1 2 3 4 5 6 7 8 9

Conductor of Group 1: When all groups have reached zero, give
a signal to reverse the count.

Groups:
- Begin with a silence for one beat.
- Make your assigned sound for four beats.
- Count silently for two beats; then repeat your sound.
- Continue sounds and silences until you reach the original number of silent beats given in your score.
- Drop out.

The composition is finished when all groups are silent.
When was the composition the loudest? softest?
How were "loud" and "soft" achieved?

AFTER HOURS

by John Pfeiffer

Listen to this music performed on an electronic synthesizer.
Describe how the composer uses:

different timbres   **dynamics**

sounds and silence

rhythmic ideas   *melodic ideas*

What does the composer mean by his title "After Hours"?
Create a composition expressing "After Hours" in another place.

Tape sounds of percussion instruments or voices.
Tape white noise (static) off the radio.
Alter these sounds by playing them back at different speeds.

JUDY'S SONG

Words and Music by Malvina Reynolds

This song does not have any expressive markings written into the score. If you were the composer, which of the following markings would you use?

pp   *mp*   *f*

andante   moderato   presto
marcato   legato   ritard.   accel.

How can the words, the rhythm, and the shape of the melody help you decide?

I've got a song, It's a-bout so high, It's a-bout this big a-
I've got a song, It's a shade of green, Em-broid-ered all o-ver with

round, It's got a won-der-ful sound,   But I can't sing it.
birds, But I don't know the words,   So I can't

sing it.   Some day I'll get on a mount-ain-top and

o-pen up my mouth, and this great big song will come rol-ling out and

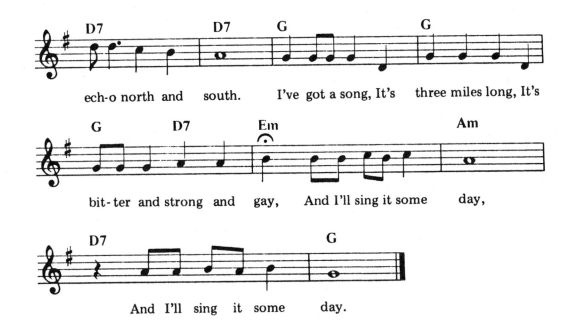

ech-o north and   south.   I've got a song, It's   three miles long, It's

bit-ter and strong and   gay,   And I'll sing it some   day,

And I'll   sing   it some   day.

Chattering cheetahs?
Bewitched, scratching
chasing
and
chopping
and scarily
thrashing!

Grinches
who
twitch
and
mew
and
pitch
over
the
chimney . . .
snicker and snitch!

BEHIND THE MOON

by B. A.

hool-mool
GROAN MOAN
Long~Hollow
LONE~LONE

I MAY NOT PASS THIS WAY AGAIN

Words and Music by Rod McKuen

Follow the expression marks as you sing.

Moderately (♩ = 90)

mp
1. I'm on my way____ to find a friend, ____

mf
And I may not pass this way a - gain. ____

f marcato
So let's to build the bridg - es, mis - ter;

f
Let's go pick the flow - ers, sis - ter.

mf   *ritard.*
Come a - long, strang - er, come a - long friend,

mp
I may not pass this way a - gain. ____

2. I'm off to find that journey's end,
   And I may not pass this way again.
   So let's go run the ridges, mister;
   Let's go find the rainbow, sister.
   Refrain

3. Let's live the day until its end,
   'Cause we may not pass this way again.
   So let's go climb the mountains, mister;
   Drink from a bubblin' fountain, sister.
   Refrain

NZOMBI
(MUSIC FOR THE RETURN FROM A HUNT)

Aka Pygmy Song

The Aka Pygmies practice an unusual musical art.
They perform duets with themselves! They sing while playing
wind instruments. Listen to "Music for the Return from a Hunt."
Can you tell when the performer is singing and when he is playing?
Notice that the performer always returns to the **same pitch**
on his **mobeke** while singing a melody that moves around this pitch.

A Duet with Myself

Try performing as the Aka Pygmies do.
Learn the melody on the next page, "The Farmer Is the Man."
Play the pitch to which the melody returns most often.
Sing all other pitches!

THE FARMER IS THE MAN

Midwestern Folk Song

Before learning the melody of this song, practice the rhythm.

Establish the tonal center by playing these chords on the autoharp.

G	C	D7	G
I	IV	V7	I

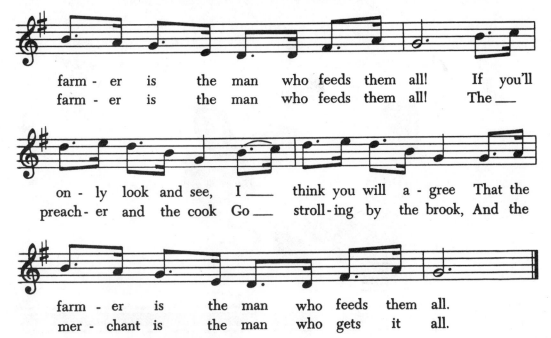

1. When the farm-er comes to town, With his wag-on bro-ken down, Oh, the
2. The __ doc-tor hangs a-round While the black-smith heats his iron, Oh, the

farm - er   is   the   man   who feeds   them   all!   If   you'll
farm - er   is   the   man   who feeds   them   all!   The __

on - ly   look   and   see,   I __   think   you   will   a - gree   That the
preach- er   and   the   cook   Go __   stroll-ing   by   the   brook,   And the

farm - er   is   the   man   who   feeds   them   all.
mer - chant   is   the   man   who   gets   it   all.

≡ A TONAL CHALLENGE ≡

Challenge a friend.
Who can best remember the tonal center of a song?
1. Choose a song you both know well.
2. Establish tonality on the autoharp.
   Play **I, IV, V7, I** in the **key** of the song.
3. **Player No. 1:** Sing or play the melody.
   Pause at the end of each phrase.
4. **Player No. 2:** When the melody pauses, sing the
   tonal center.

Example:

Skip to My Lou

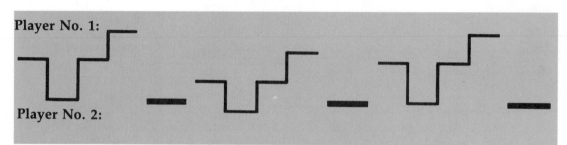

5. **Self check:** Check by playing the tonal center on bells.
6. **Point system:** Player 2 gets one point each time the tonal
   center is sung correctly.
7. Trade jobs; try again.

ON SPRINGFIELD MOUNTAIN

American Folk Song

When you can't play the chords on an instrument, establish the tonal center by using another method.

Play the **E major** scale on the bells: E, F♯, G♯, A, B, C♯, D♯, E

1. On Spring-field Moun - tain there did dwell
2. On Fri - day morn - ing he did go
3. When he re - ceived his death - ly wound,

A hand - some youth, was known full well,
Down to the mead - ows for to mow,
He laid his scythe up - on the ground,

Lieu - ten - ant Mer - rill's on - ly son,
He mowed, he mowed all round the field
For to re - turn was his in - tent,

A like - ly youth, full twen - ty - one.
With a poi - son-ous sar - pent at his heel.
Call - ing a - loud a-long as he went.

4. Day being past, night coming on,
   The father went to seek his son,
   And there he found his only son,
   Cold as a stone, dead on the ground.

5. He took him up and he carried him home,
   And on the way did weep and mourn,
   Saying, "I heard, but did not come,
   And now I'm left alone to mourn."

≡ A "MINOR" CHALLENGE ≡

You have been testing your ability to remember the tonal
center in songs based on a **major scale**.
Try a new problem.
"Shalom Chaverim" is based on a **minor scale**.
Sing a minor scale:

Play the game as before:
- The first person sings or plays each pattern.
- The second person must sing the tonal center at the
  end of each pattern.
- The second person checks by playing E on the bells.

≡ SHALOM CHAVERIM ≡
≡ (FAREWELL, GOOD FRIENDS) ≡

Israeli Round

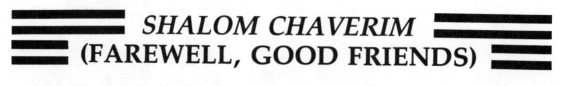

Sha - lom, cha - ve - rim! Sha - lom, cha - ve - rim! Sha - lom, sha - lom!
Fare - well, good _ friends, Fare - well, good _ friends, Fare - well, fare - well!

Le - hit - ra - ot, le - hit - ra - ot, Sha - lom, sha - lom!
Till we meet a - gain, till we meet a - gain, Fare - well, fare - well!

MACARONI (I MACCHERONI)

English Words Adapted

Neapolitan Folk Song

Tune up by playing and singing this form of the minor scale.

Tempo of Tarantella

Boys

1. I'm so poor, hear what I'm say - in,' I've no
2. I would like to be a sol - dier In the
3. My lieu - ten - ant, oh, so ar - dent, Changed his

Girls

bed nor place to stay in. You'd best sell your shirt for
ar - my, like I told 'ya. Push the can - non, pull the
place with his own ser - geant. Sold his rank to get your

mon - ey, 'Fat - ten you up with mac - a - ro - ni.
po - ny, Still buy a dish of mac - a - ro - ni.
mon - ey; Now he will eat your mac - a - ro - ni.

Together

Ven - de - rei i miei cal - zo - ni, Per un sol

piat - to di mac - che - ro - ni.

ERIE CANAL

American Work Song

Play the recording.
Which part of the song is based on a minor scale?

Which part of the song is based on a major scale?

Try this challenge:
> One person controls the volume knob on the phonograph.
> As the recording is played, turn the volume to soft
> just before the singer reaches the last note of each
> two-measure phrase.
> The class must then sing the **tonal center,**
> not the last note of the phrase!

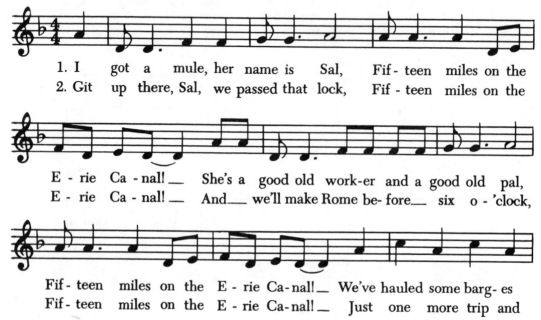

1. I got a mule, her name is Sal, Fif-teen miles on the
2. Git up there, Sal, we passed that lock, Fif-teen miles on the

E-rie Ca-nal! __ She's a good old work-er and a good old pal,
E-rie Ca-nal! __ And__ we'll make Rome be-fore__ six o-'clock,

Fif-teen miles on the E-rie Ca-nal! __ We've hauled some barg-es
Fif-teen miles on the E-rie Ca-nal! __ Just one more trip and

in our day, Filled with lum-ber, coal, and hay, And we know ev - ery
back we'll go Through the rain and sleet and snow,'Cause we know ev - ery

inch of the way From Al - ba - ny __ to __ Buf - fa - lo. ____
inch of the way From Al - ba - ny __ to __ Buf - fa - lo. ____

Refrain

Low bridge, ev- ery-bod-y down, Low bridge,'cause we're com-ing to a town;

And you'll al - ways know your neigh-bor, You'll al-ways know your pal,

If you ev - er nav - i - gat - ed on the E - rie Ca - nal. __

Play the following scales on the bells.
Some are written with mistakes.
In each scale with a mistake, give the number of the scale
step that is wrong.

Scale steps	1	2	3	4	5	6	7	1'
	C	D	E	F	G	A	B	C
	D	E	F#	G#	A	B	C#	D
Scales	E♭	F#	G	A	B♭	C	D	E♭
	F	G	A	B♭	C	D	E	F
	G	A	B	C	D	E	F	G

Can you correct the scales that have an error?
Why do you suppose you can recognize these mistakes?
Find out by working in pairs or small groups to complete
the guide sheet, "A Scale Is a Scale Is a Major Scale."

▤ A Scale Is to a Melody... ▤

Can you name this familiar song by reading the scale numbers?

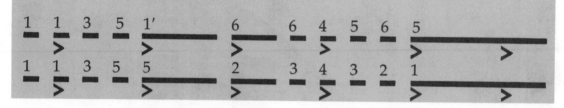

Play it using one of the correct scales in the chart above.
Play it again, using one of the incorrect scales.
Discuss the relationship of "A scale is to a melody . . ."

52

MASQUERADE SUITE
Waltz

by Aram Khachaturian

Listen to this composition. It has several melodies, each of
which makes exciting music for a whirling waltz.

1	**Introduction**	The music sets the mood for waltzing.
2	**A** (repeated)	The first melody moves from high to low. Listen for the echo patterns.
3	**B** (repeated)	This is a melody that sounds dark and strong.
4	**A**	
5	Interlude	Brass plays rhythmic pattern, first loud, then soft, in preparation for the next theme.
6	**C**	This is a light, happy melody. Listen for the crisp sounds of the woodwinds, and then for the brass instruments as they climb the scale.
7	**?**	Which section do you hear? A or B?
8	**B**	Listen for the which help to accent the music.
9	**A**	The opening melody returns and is the last to be heard. The composition ends with a slight ritard and a crash of the cymbals on the final chord.

SCRAMBLED SCALES

Can you sing a major scale with scale numbers?
If you can, you can sing a melody with scale numbers,
because a melody is just a scrambled-up scale!
Sing these phrases from familiar songs.
If you sing them correctly you will know the **titles.**

Title??

G is the tonal **center.**

| 3 | 4 | 5 | 6 | 5 | 3 | 1 | 3 | 4 | 5 | 6 | 5 | 3 | 1 |

Title??

C is the tonal **center.**

| 5 | 5 | 1' | 1' | 1' | 1' | 1' | 1' | 1' | 1' | 7 | 7 | 7 | 7 | 7 |

Title??

F is the tonal **center.**

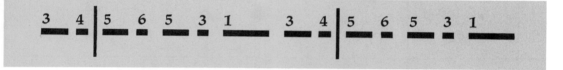

| 5₁ | 1 | 2 | 3 | 3 | 3 | 3 | 5 | 2 |

Title??

F is the tonal **center.**

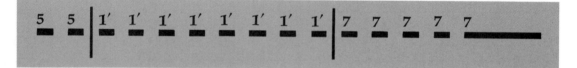

| 5 | 5 | 5 | 3 | 4 | 4 | 4 | 2 | 3 | 3 | 3 | 1 | 2 | 7₁ | 6₁ | 5₁ |

Here are the familiar melodies you sang with scale numbers.
Can you match each melody with its notation?
What clues can help you?

JOY TO THE WORLD

Words by William Wolff

Music Attributed
to George Frederic Handel

Tune Up:

Most of this melody moves by scale numbers.
Establish tonality by singing the "Tune Up."
Can you then sing the melody with scale numbers?
Tapping the shortest sound may help you sense the rhythm
of the melody.

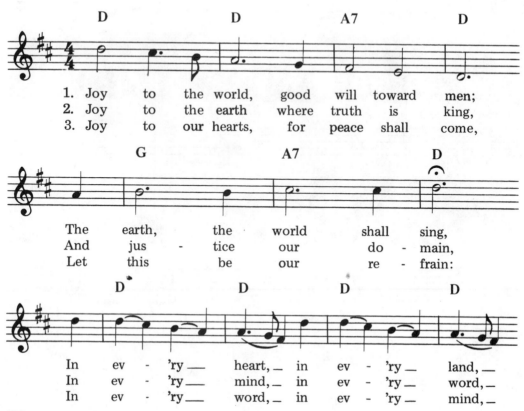

1. Joy to the world, good will toward men;
2. Joy to the earth where truth is king,
3. Joy to our hearts, for peace shall come,

The earth, the world shall sing,
And jus - tice our do - main,
Let this be our re - frain:

In ev - 'ry — heart, — in ev - 'ry — land, —
In ev - 'ry — mind, — in ev - 'ry — word, —
In ev - 'ry — word, — in ev - 'ry — mind, —

Let peace and free-dom_ ring, Let_ peace and free-dom ring,

Let_ peace and broth-er-hood and free-dom ring.

Listen to the traditional version of this song.
Does the melody sound the same?

Peaceable Kingdom

The theme of peace on earth has been expressed by many artists,
composers, and poets. Can you find other examples?

Holy Mountain III, by Horace Pippin, 1945.
Hirschorn Museum and Sculpture Garden, Smithsonian Institution.

57

IN THE PINES

Traditional

Most melodies of our culture move by

Scale Steps

or by

Chordal Skips

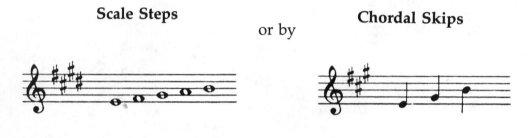

Locate the skips in this song that use tones of the **I** chord.
Establish the tonal center; sing the song with scale numbers.

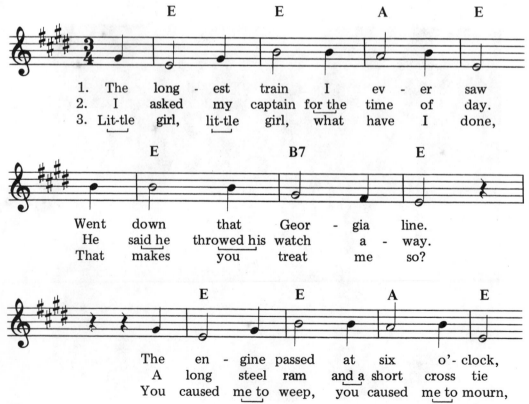

1. The long - est train I ev - er saw
2. I asked my captain for the time of day.
3. Lit-tle girl, lit-tle girl, what have I done,

Went down that Geor - gia line.
He said he throwed his watch a - way.
That makes you treat me so?

The en - gine passed at six o'- clock,
A long steel ram and a short cross tie
You caused me to weep, you caused me to mourn,

58

E B7 E
And cab passed by at nine.
I'm on my way back home.
You caused me to leave my home.

Chorus

E E A E
In the pines, in the pines, Where the sun nev-er shines,

E B7 E
And we shiv - er when the cold wind_ blows.

LA CUCARACHA

Mexican Folk Song

Find patterns that skip using tones of:

the **I** chord

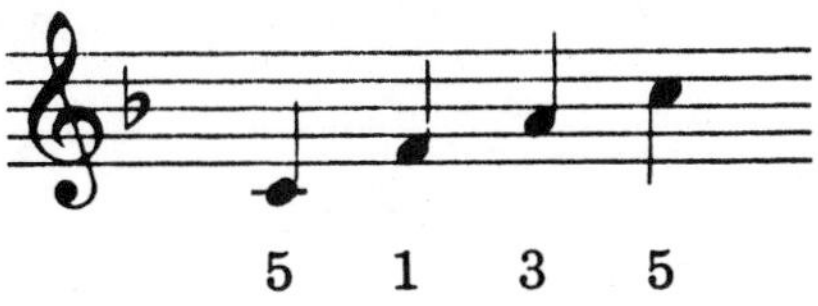

5 1 3 5

the **V** chord

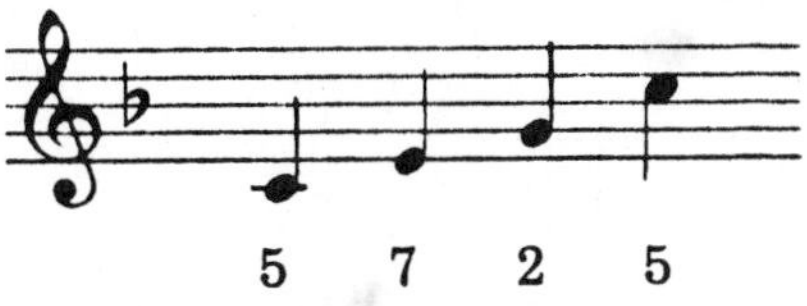

5 7 2 5

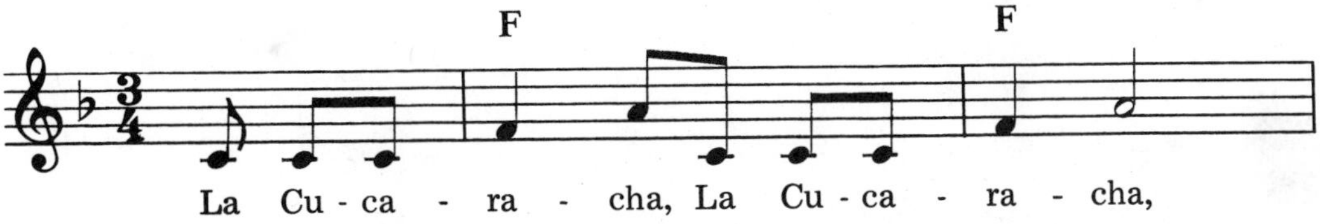

F F
La Cu - ca - ra - cha, La Cu - ca - ra - cha,

F C7 C7
he's a mer - ry lit - tle bug. La Cu-ca - ra - cha, La Cu-ca -

C7 C7 F
ra - cha, scam - per - ing a - cross the rug.

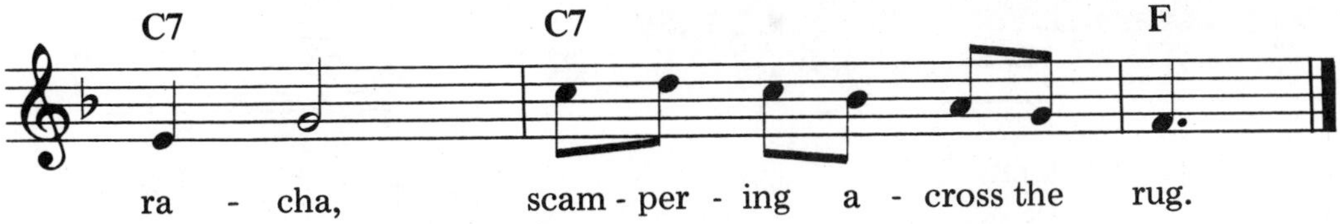

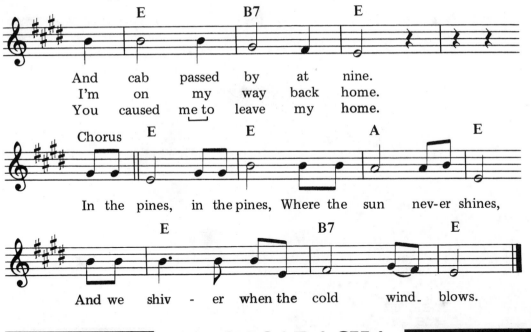

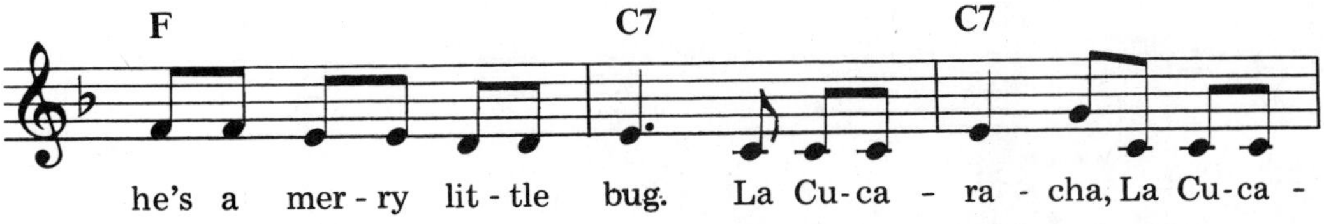

SIMPLE GIFTS

Shaker Song

Tune Up:

1 3 5 3 1 7 2 5 2 7 1

Most of this song moves by steps.
Find all the places that move by skips.
Do the skips use tones of the **I** chord, or of the **V** chord?

'Tis the gift   to be sim - ple, 'tis the gift   to be   free, 'Tis the

gift   to   come down where you ought to   be, And when we   find our-

selves   in the place just   right, 'Twill   be   in the val - ley of

love and de - light.   When   true   sim - pli - ci - ty   is   gained, To

bow   and to bend we   shan't be a - shamed, To   turn, turn will

be   our de - light, Till by turn - ing, turn - ing we come round right.

VARIATIONS ON A SHAKER TUNE

from *Appalachian Spring*

by Aaron Copland

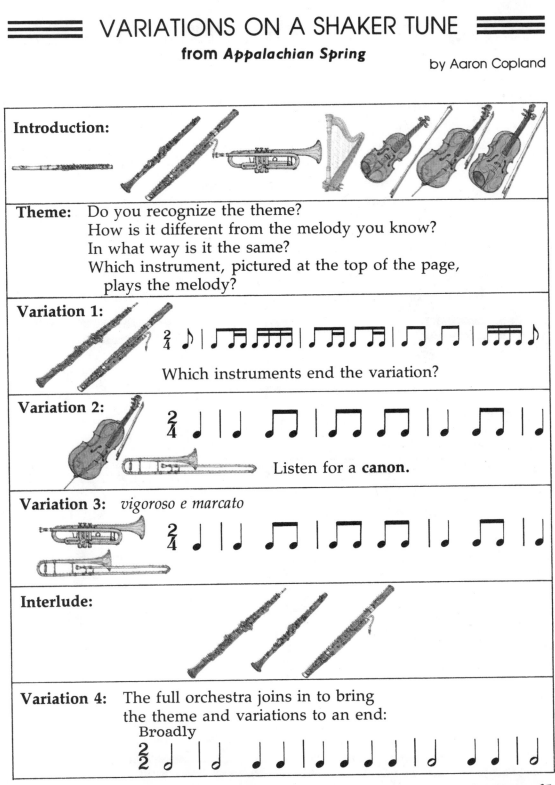

Introduction:

Theme: Do you recognize the theme?
How is it different from the melody you know?
In what way is it the same?
Which instrument, pictured at the top of the page,
plays the melody?

Variation 1:
Which instruments end the variation?

Variation 2:
Listen for a **canon.**

Variation 3: *vigoroso e marcato*

Interlude:

Variation 4: The full orchestra joins in to bring
the theme and variations to an end:
Broadly

Compose Variations

Do as Copland did.

Take a folk tune, such as "Chairs to Mend."

Play variations using some of the ideas Copland used:

Perform the rhythm in **diminution.**

Perform it in **augmentation.**

Play it in different **tempos.**

Alter the **melody.**

CHAIRS TO MEND

Traditional Round

Chairs to mend, old chairs to mend? Mack-er-el, fresh

mack-er-el! An-y old rags, an-y old rags?

CHECK YOUR MUSICAL STRENGTH (2)

SHENANDOAH

American Sea Chantey

Oh, Shen-an-doah, — I long to hear you
Oh, Shen-an-doah, — I love your daugh-ter,
Oh, Shen-an-doah, — I'm bound to leave you,

A way, you roll-in' riv-er,

Oh, Shen-an-doah, — I long to hear you,
Oh, Shen-an-doah, — I love your daugh-ter,
Oh, Shen-an-doah, — I'm bound to leave you,

A - way I'm bound to go, 'Cross the wide Mis - sour - i.

Can you:

- perform a song with suitable expression?
- hear and identify the tonal center of a song?
- hear the differences between major and minor?
- find the pitches of a major scale?
- read and perform melodies that move by steps and chordal skips?
- create variations on a tune?

63

DINAH

Traditional

Some-one's in the kit - chen with Di – nah,

Some-one's in the kit - chen with Di – nah,

Some-one's in the kit - chen I know, _____

Some-one's in the kit - chen I know,

Some-one's in the kit - chen with Di – nah,

Some-one's in the kit - chen with Di – nah,

Strum-ming on the old ban - jo.

Strum-ming on the old ban - jo.

64

LOCATING TONAL CENTERS: SHARPS

The songs on pages 64 and 66 are each based on a different **tonal center.**

Can you discover the tonal center for each?

The information is contained in the **key signature.**

To help you solve this problem, make a chart of the scales listed below. Follow the same steps used when doing the activity "A Scale Is a Scale Is a Major Scale," page 52.

Scale	1	2	3	4	5	6	7	1	sharped letters	sharped steps
	G									
	D									
	A									
	E									

Use the information in the chart to match each scale with its key signature.

Make a rule for finding tonal centers of key signatures using sharps. You will need to know the names of the lines and spaces. If you are not sure, look at the back cover of your book.

WHIPPOORWILL ROUND

Traditional

1. Gone to bed is the set-ting sun,

2. Night is com-ing and day is done, Whip-poor-

3. will, whip-poor-will, has just ___ be-gun.

THE SILVER MOON IS SHINING

Italian Folk Song

1. The sil - ver moon is shin - ing Up -
2. The night - in - gale is sing - ing Be -

on the si - lent mead - ow, I walk a - down the
yond the for - est shad - ow, I sigh with - in the

mead - ow with no one near me.
shad - ow where none can hear me.

CHESTER

from *New England Triptych*

by William Schuman

Can you learn the melody below by reading scale numbers?
It is based on the **D Major scale.**

William Schuman, an American composer, used this melody as
the basis for an instrumental composition. Follow the notation of
the theme as it is passed from instrument to instrument.

Discuss the differences between what you hear and what you see.

Make copies of the theme.
Draw pictures of the instruments.
Use the illustrations on pages 88, 89, and 90 as your guide.
Combine instruments and notation to make your own Music Map.

LOCATING THE TONAL CENTERS: FLATS

The songs on pages 68, 69, and 70 have key signatures with flats.

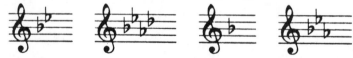

Write out each scale. Prepare a rule for locating tonal centers when flats are in the key signature.

Scale	1	2	3	4	5	6	7	1'	flatted letters	flatted scale steps
	F									
	B♭									
	E♭									
	A♭									

BUON GIORNO

Italian Round

After you have learned the melody, listen to the recording to learn the Italian words.

Buon gior - no, mi - a   ca - ra   bam - bi - na,   mol - ti ba - ci,

Buon gior - no, mi - a   ca - ra   bam - bi - na,   mol - ti ba - ci,

Buon gior - no, mi - a   ca - ra   bam - bi - na,   mol - ti ba - ci!

A HORSE NAMED BILL

Words by Jerry Silverman

Adapted from Dan Emmett's *Dixie*

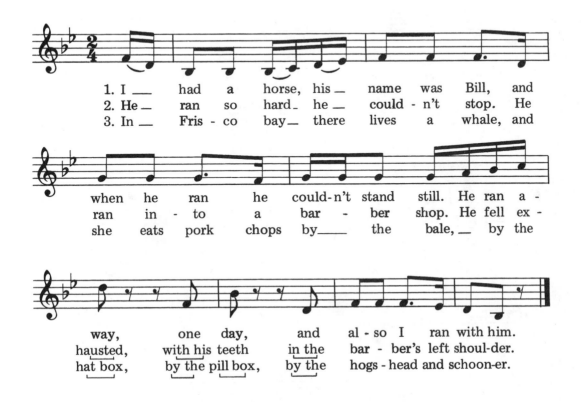

1. I __ had a horse, his __ name was Bill, and when he ran he could-n't stand still. He ran a-way, one day, and al-so I ran with him.

2. He __ ran so hard __ he __ could-n't stop. He ran in-to a bar - ber shop. He fell ex-hausted, with his teeth in the bar - ber's left shoul-der.

3. In __ Fris - co bay __ there lives a whale, and she eats pork chops by __ the bale, __ by the hat box, by the pill box, by the hogs - head and schoon-er.

DONKEY RIDING

Canadian Folk Song

1. Were you ev - er in Que - bec, Stow - ing tim - ber
2. Were you ev - er in Car - diff Bay, Where the folks all

on a deck, Where there's a king with a
shout "Hoo - ray! Here comes__ John with his

gold - en crown, Rid - ing on a don - key?
three months' pay, Rid - ing on a don - key."

Refrain

Hey - ho! A - way we go! Don - key rid - ing, don - key rid - ing,

Hey - ho! A - way we go, Rid - ing on a don - key!

MYSTERY TUNES

Can you name this mystery tune?
Follow these scale numbers, playing in **D Major.**
What bells will you need?

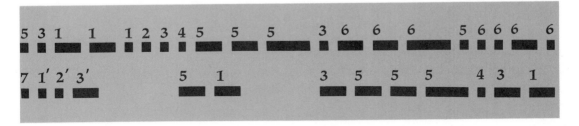

Now play it using a different scale. Choose one from the chart below.

1. Select a starting pitch.
2. Arrange the bells in the order of whole and half steps as shown in the chart.
3. Add extra bells above 1′ as needed.
4. Play the tune by following the same scale numbers.
5. What happens to the sound of the melody?

Major Scale	X		X		X	X		X		X		X	X
Minor Scale	X		X	X		X		X	X		X		X
Whole tone	X		X		X		X		X		X		X
Mixolydian	X		X		X	X		X		X	X		X
Dorian	X		X	X		X		X		X	X		X

Choose another tune you know well.
Write it out in scale numbers.
Play it using a different scale from that on which it is based.
Play it for your friends.
Can they guess the mystery tune?

OLD JOE CLARKE

American Folk Song

Locate all the different pitches used in this song.
Begin with the tonal center F.
Write the pitches in order from low to high.
Arrange the pitches on a chart to show the whole and half steps.
Look at the scales on page 71. Which pattern does this scale match?

1. Old Joe Clarke he had a house Six-teen sto-ries high;
2. I went down to Old Joe's house, nev-er been there be-fore;

Ev - ery sto - ry in that house Was filled with chick-en pie.
He slept on a feath-er bed And I slept on the floor.

Refrain
Round and round, Old Joe Clarke, Round and round I say;

Round and round, Old Joe Clarke, I have-n't long to stay.

SCARBOROUGH FAIR

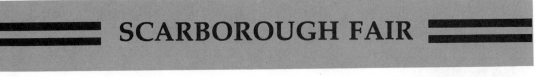

English Folk Song

Follow the same method used in learning "Old Joe Clarke."
Can you choose the scale for this song?

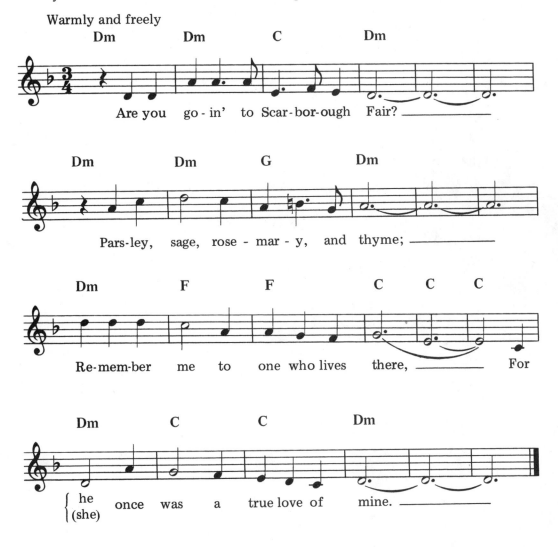

THE SEA

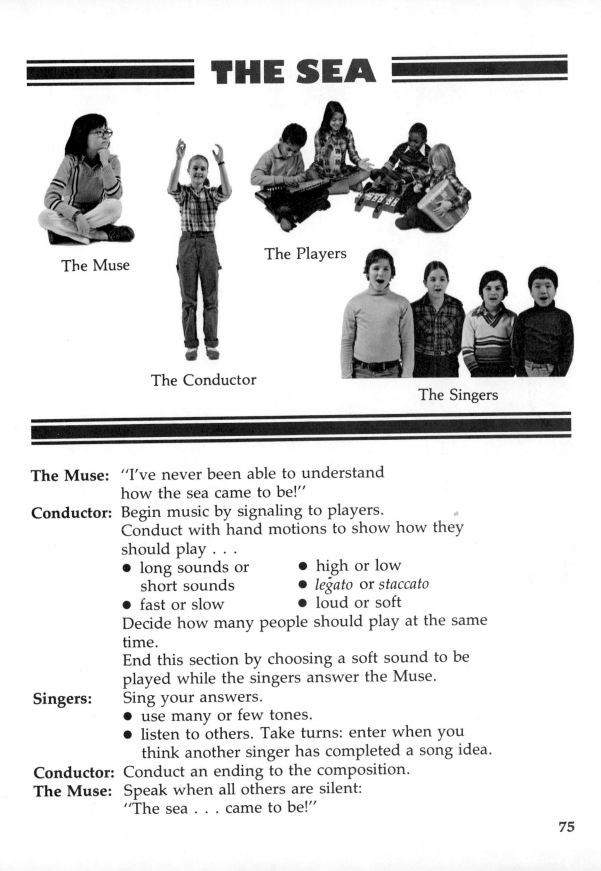

The Muse

The Conductor

The Players

The Singers

The Muse: "I've never been able to understand how the sea came to be!"

Conductor: Begin music by signaling to players.
Conduct with hand motions to show how they should play . . .
- long sounds or short sounds
- fast or slow
- high or low
- *legato* or *staccato*
- loud or soft

Decide how many people should play at the same time.
End this section by choosing a soft sound to be played while the singers answer the Muse.

Singers: Sing your answers.
- use many or few tones.
- listen to others. Take turns: enter when you think another singer has completed a song idea.

Conductor: Conduct an ending to the composition.

The Muse: Speak when all others are silent:
"The sea . . . came to be!"

75

IMPROVISATION ON WHOLE TONES

Set up your mallet instruments to use these tones:
Soprano Glockenspiel or Resonator Bells

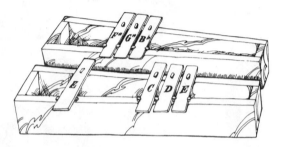

Alto Xylophone   Bass Metallophone

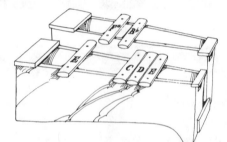   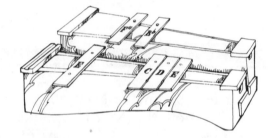

A Section
Glockenspiel plays a descending pattern in this rhythm:

Xylophone and metallophone take turns answering with
  a single tone   a chord   another descending pattern

B Section
Glockenspiel plays ascending *glissandi* by scraping
mallet across all bells:

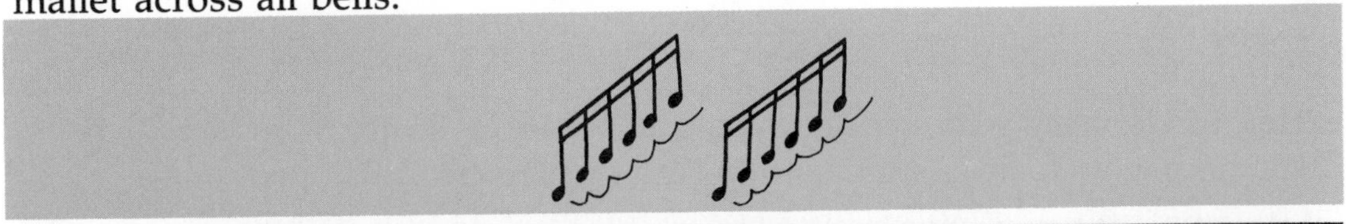

Metallophone answers with large skips:

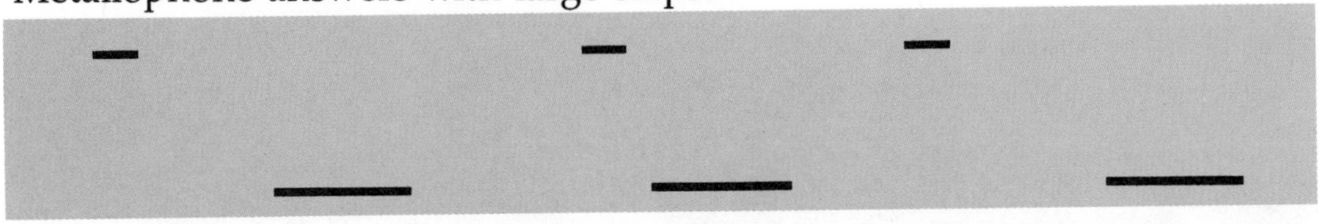

C Section
Alto xylophone improvises melody:

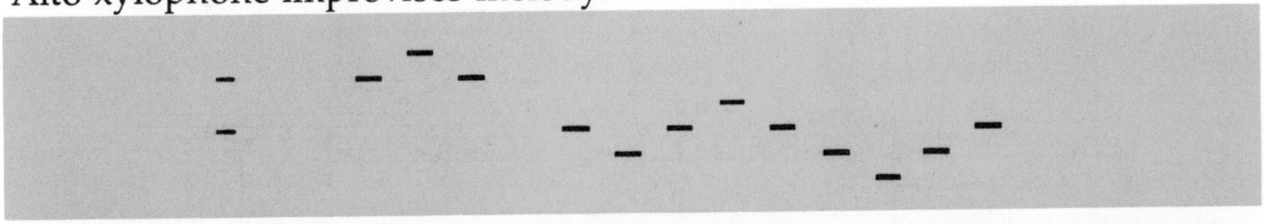

Metallophone accompanies with ascending long tones:

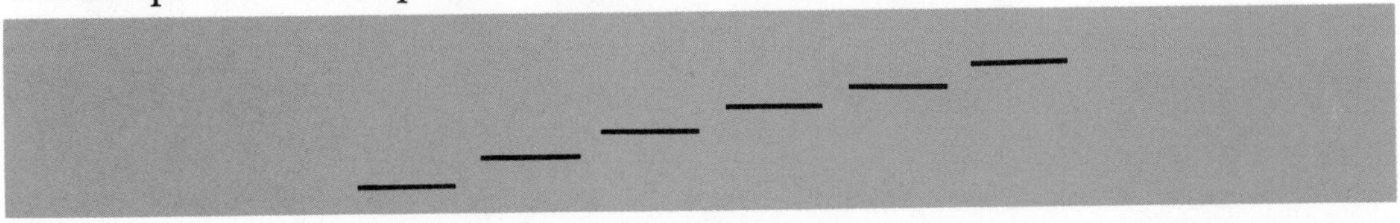

Combine the three sections in any order you like
to make a complete composition.

77

VOILES

by Claude Debussy

Listen to Debussy's composition on a whole-tone scale.
Does he use any ideas similar to the ones on page 76?
Here is part of the piano score. Try to follow it as you listen.
Can you tell when each of these sections is played?
Are any of the ideas repeated?

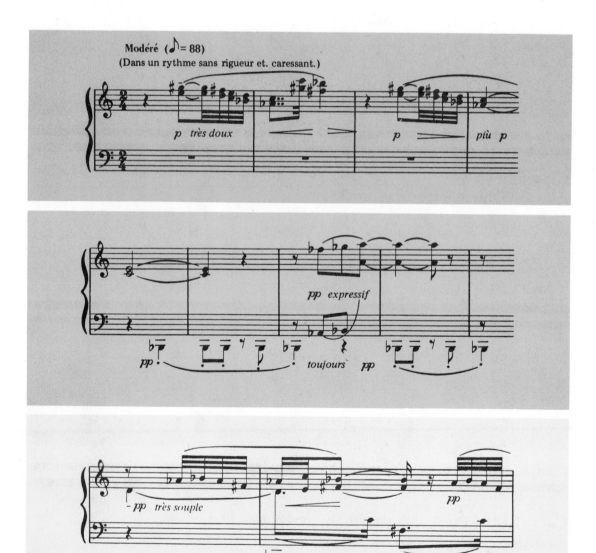

Voiles means "sails," as used on sailing ships. What kind of ship scene might Debussy have been suggesting?

What name would you give to your whole-tone composition? Did you get ideas from Debussy's music that will help you improve yours?

BINGO

German Folk Song
Arranged by David J. Riley

Tap the shortest unit of sound while singing this familiar song.
Sing first in unison, then as a round.

Da war ein Bauer mit ein - em Hunde und Bin - go war sein
There was a farm - er had a dog and Bin - go was his

Na - me,⎰
name - o,⎱

B - I - N-G-O, B - I - N-G-O,

B - I - N-G-O ⎰und Bin - go war sein Na - me.
⎱and Bin - go was his name - o.

Each time you repeat the song, drop one letter from the name
BINGO. Replace the letter with sounds such as:

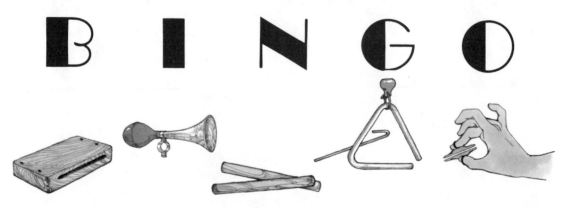

Select two musicians and three groups of dancers.

Bongo Player:

Bell Player: Create three different patterns. Each should last four measures:

1. Use only the shortest sounds. ♪♪

2. Use sounds that are twice as long. ♩

3. Use sounds that are four times as long. 𝅗𝅥

Use these bells:

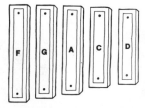

Create a composition by alternating among the three patterns. Continue the composition by repeating the patterns in any order.

Dancers: Group 1: Move when you hear pattern 1.
Group 2: Move when you hear pattern 2.
Group 3: Move when you hear pattern 3.
Move only when you hear your assigned pattern.
Freeze when any other patterns are played.
Begin in special areas, then move
together in one large area.

≡≡ A CHALLENGE GAME ≡≡

Here is a challenge to your listening skills.
Can you identify the rhythm pattern you hear in relation
to the shortest unit of sound?
Look as you listen.
Call out the number of the pattern you hear.

1.

Rhythm

Shortest sound

2.

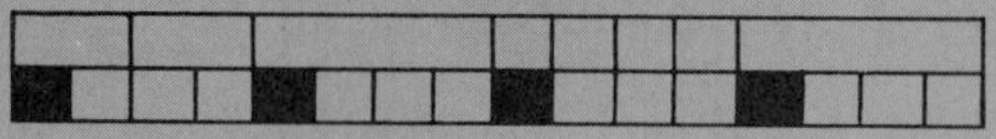

Rhythm

Shortest sound

3.

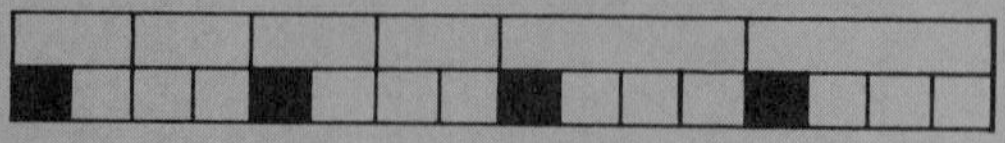

Rhythm

Shortest sound

4.

Rhythm

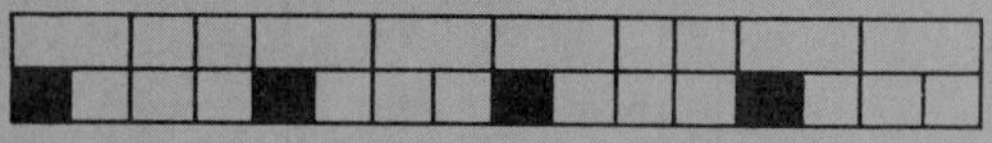

Shortest sound

Can you now tap each pattern?

TOEMBAÏ

Israeli Round

Tune Up:

Compare the patterns you see in this song with the ones you
heard when playing the Challenge Game.
Can you match each pattern with its notation?
Establish an *andante* tempo.
Tap the shortest unit of sound. Chant the words of the
song rhythmically.

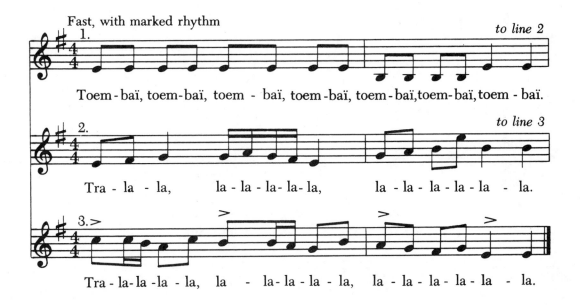

Learn the melody. Will you establish tonality in major or
in minor? When you know the melody, establish an
allegro tempo.
Sing the song.

GUANTANAMERA
(LADY OF GUANTANAMO)

Spanish Words by José Martí
English Adaptation by Bernard Gasso

Traditional

Read and play these instrumental parts.
1. Play the shortest sounds.
2. How does the beat move in relation to the shortest sounds?
   Play the beat and the shortest sounds together.
3. How does the rhythm pattern move in relation to the shortest sounds?
   Play the rhythm pattern and the shortest sounds together.

Play the three parts while singing the song.

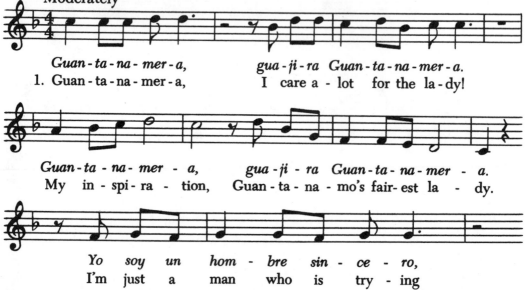

Guan - ta - na - mer - a, gua - ji - ra Guan - ta - na - mer - a.
1. Guan - ta - na - mer - a, I care a - lot for the la - dy!

Guan - ta - na - mer - a, gua - ji - ra Guan - ta - na - mer - a.
My in - spi - ra - tion, Guan - ta - na - mo's fair - est la - dy.

Yo soy un hom - bre sin - ce - ro,
I'm just a man who is try - ing

de don - de cre - ce la ___ pal - ma, ___
To do some good be - fore ___ dy - ing, ___

Yo soy un hom - bre sin - ce - ro,
To ask each man and his broth - er

de don - de cre - ce la pal - ma, ___
To bear no ill ___ toward each oth - er. ___

Ya n tes de mor - rir - me quie - ro,
This life will nev - er be hol - low

E - char mis ver - sos del al - ma.
To those who lis - ten and fol - low.

Guan - ta - na - mer - a, gua - ji - ra Guan - ta - na - mer - a.
Guan - ta - na - mer - a, I care a - lot for the la - dy!

Guan - ta - na - mer - a, gua - ji - ra Guan - ta - na - mer - a.
My in - spi - ra - tion, Guan - ta - na - mo's fair - est la - dy.

BOSTON COME-ALL-YE

Sea Chantey

Look at the **meter signature** at the beginning of the song.
Does the **meter signature** give information about the beat?
shortest sound? rhythm pattern of the melody?

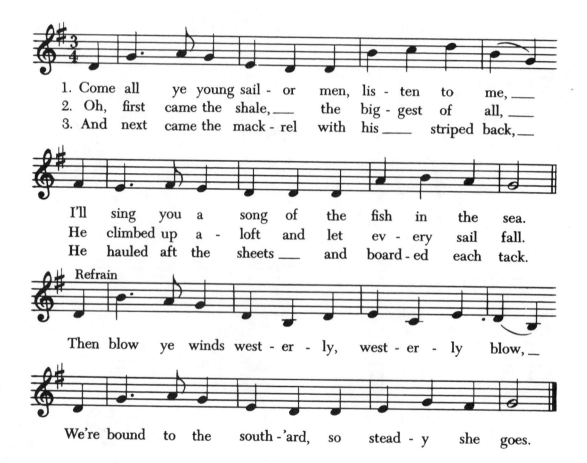

1. Come all ye young sail - or men, lis - ten to me, ___
2. Oh, first came the shale, ___ the big - gest of all, ___
3. And next came the mack - rel with his ___ striped back, ___

I'll sing you a song of the fish in the sea.
He climbed up a - loft and let ev - ery sail fall.
He hauled aft the sheets ___ and board - ed each tack.

Refrain

Then blow ye winds west - er - ly, west - er - ly blow, ___

We're bound to the south -'ard, so stead - y she goes.

4. Then came the smelt, the smallest of all;
   He jumped to the poop and sang out, "Top-sail haul!"
   Then blow ye . . .

5. Last came the flounder, as flat as the ground,
   Says, "Blast your eyes, chuckle-head, mind how you sound!"
   Then blow ye . . .

CHECK YOUR MUSICAL STRENGTH (3)

SANDY McNAB

Traditional Round

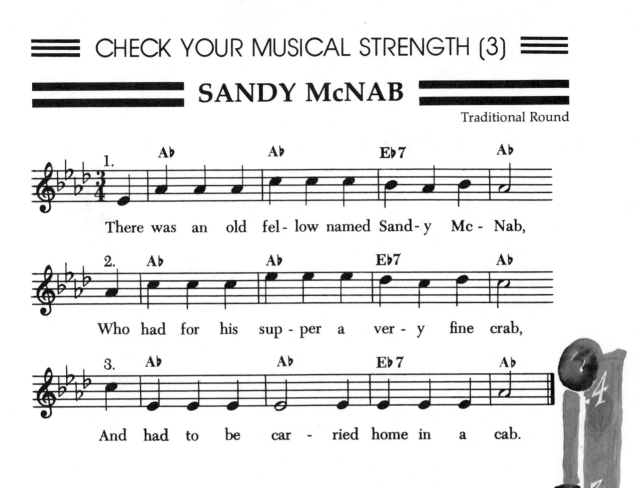

1. | A♭ | A♭ | E♭7 | A♭ |

There was an old fel-low named Sand-y Mc-Nab,

2. | A♭ | A♭ | E♭7 | A♭ |

Who had for his sup-per a ver-y fine crab,

3. | A♭ | A♭ | E♭7 | A♭ |

And had to be car - ried home in a cab.

Can you:
- find the tonal center of the song "Sandy McNab" by looking at the key signature?
- tell what scale the melody uses?
- learn to sing "Sandy McNab" by reading the music notation?
- create an *ostinato* accompaniment for this song?
- play a musical game?

A COMPOSER AND THE ORCHESTRA

When a composer writes music, many decisions must be made. One important decision a composer makes is the choice of instruments to perform each part.

If you were a composer, how would you decide which instrument should play the main melody? the harmonizing parts? What would you think about as you made your choices?

Listen to a composer, Howard Hanson, discuss the instruments of the orchestra and explain some of the ways he chooses the instruments for his compositions.

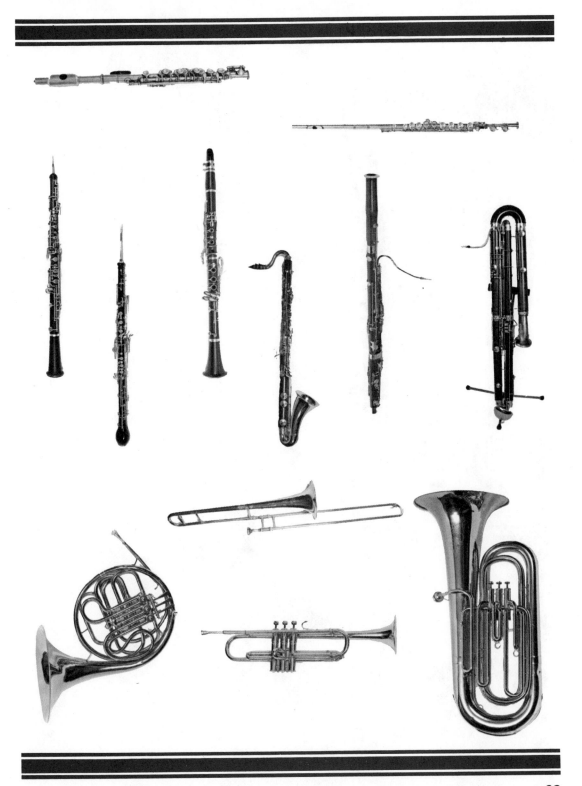

CHILDREN'S DANCE
from *Merry Mount Suite*

by Howard Hanson

Listen to the "Children's Dance" in its entirety.
Can you identify the instruments and the part each plays?
Try to imagine how this music would have sounded if the
composer had selected different instruments for each part.

Your Own Composition for Orchestra

Plan a performance of "America for Me, for Orchestra."
The parts have been prepared for you on charts.
Make a list of the instruments class members play:

- instruments played in music class
- instruments studied privately
- instruments studied in the school instrumental program.

Think about these questions as you plan your performance:

- Which instrumentalists can play each part?
- Are the parts in a key that will sound "right" on
  that instrument when played with others?
- Which instruments should play the melody? the
  harmony?

Experiment with different combinations of instruments.
Choose a conductor. Rehearse the composition.
Play it for another class.

SING THAT CHORD PATTERN!

Prepare three sets of game cards for each of these chords:

| I | IV | V | V7 |

Set 1: Make up patterns that begin on the **root** of each chord:

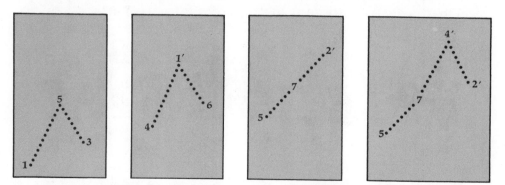

Set 2: Make up patterns that begin on the **third** (the second note) of each chord:

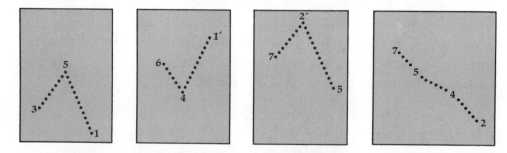

Set 3: Make up patterns that begin on the **fifth** (the third note) of each chord:

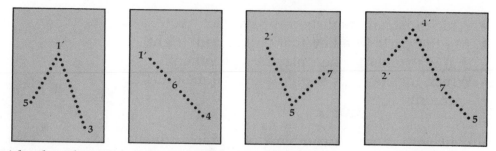

Divide the class into two teams, "The Sharps" and "The Flats." Play the game "Sing That Chord Pattern!"

92

Rules:

1. Player 1 from The Sharps
   - chooses a chord: **I, IV, V,** or **V7,**
   - chooses a set: 1, 2, or 3,
   - draws a card from that set.

2. The leader, or a player, from the opposite team plays the chosen chords.

3. Player 1 sings the pattern. Three attempts may be made.

4. If Player 1 of The Sharps misses the pattern, Player 1 of The Flats may have one try.

5. It is now the turn of the first player of The Flats.

6. Continue until every player has had at least one turn.
   To Score:
   Give points according to the difficulty of the pattern chosen.

Point Chart

	Set 1	Set 2	Set 3
I Chord	1	4	7
V Chord	2	5	8
IV Chord	3	6	9
V7 Chord	4	7	10

ONE BOTTLE OF POP

Traditional
Arranged by Marie Winn

Tune Up:

Each measure uses the **root** of a chord.
Can you name each chord?

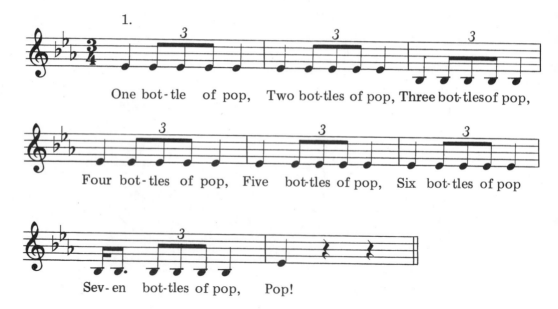

1.
One bot-tle of pop, Two bot-tles of pop, Three bot-tles of pop,

Four bot-tles of pop, Five bot-tles of pop, Six bot-tles of pop

Sev-en bot-tles of pop, Pop!

Which measures of the next melody are based on tones of the
I chord? the **V7** chord?

Do they match those of the first melody?

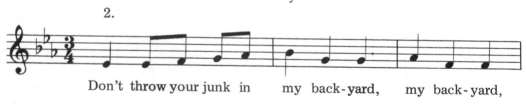

2.
Don't throw your junk in my back-yard, my back-yard,

my   back - yard,   Don't throw your junk in   my   back - yard,

My   back - yard's   full.

The third melody moves by scale steps.

Can you accompany it with the same chord sequence used for
the first two melodies?

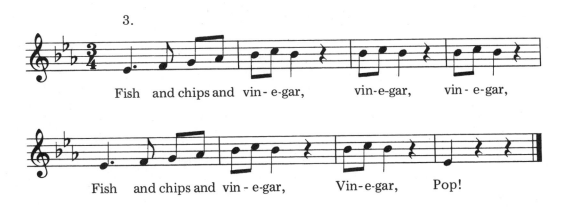

3.

Fish   and chips and vin - e-gar,   vin-e-gar,   vin - e-gar,

Fish   and chips and vin - e-gar,   Vin-e-gar,   Pop!

Divide the class into three groups.
Sing the three melodies as a "triplet" song!
Can you describe the difference between a partner song and a
triplet song?

SINGING
THE ROOT BASS

When you sang "Bottle of Pop" as a triplet song,
Group 1 was singing the root of each chord.

You can add harmony to other songs by singing the roots.
Try these songs. When will you use each root?

Skip to My Lou

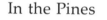

I   V

Dobbin, Dobbin

I   V

In the Pines

I IV V

Add a "jug" accompaniment:

- Get two plastic jugs.
- Practice blowing across the opening until you can get a sound.
- Add water to one until you get two tones that are five steps apart.
- The lower sound will be the root for the **I** chord.
- The higher sound will be the root for the **V7** chord.

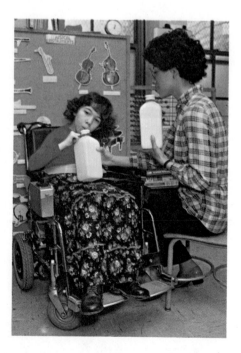

ON TOP OF OLD SMOKY

Kentucky Folk Song

Play **I, IV, V7, I** in the key of **C: C, F, G7, C.**
Plan an accompaniment for this melody.
How will you decide when to use each chord?

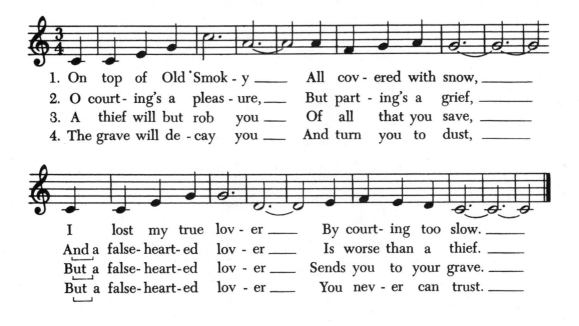

1. On top of Old ˙Smok - y _____ All cov - ered with snow, _____
2. O court - ing's a pleas - ure, ___ But part - ing's a grief, _____
3. A thief will but rob you ___ Of all that you save, _____
4. The grave will de - cay you ___ And turn you to dust, _____

I lost my true lov - er _____ By court - ing too slow. _____
And a false - heart - ed lov - er _____ Is worse than a thief. _____
But a false - heart - ed lov - er _____ Sends you to your grave. _____
But a false - heart - ed lov - er _____ You nev - er can trust. _____

Add a vocal accompaniment.
Sing the "root bass" or any other pitch from the
accompanying chords:

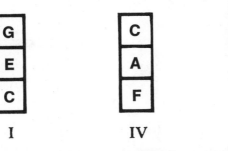

SING THAT CHORD PATTERN—TOGETHER

Play the game "Sing That Chord Pattern" again, but in a new way.
Divide into teams of four.

1. Choose a chord: **I, IV,** or **V7.**
2. Choose a set: set 1, 2, or 3.
3. Draw a card.

To sing: each member of the team sings a pitch and holds until all are sounded.

Example

I chord, set 2

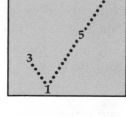

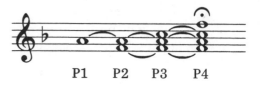

P1 P2 P3 P4

V7 chord, set 1

P1 P2 P3 P4

IV chord, set 3

P1 P2 P3 P4

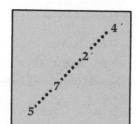

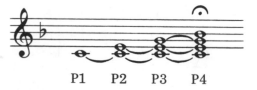

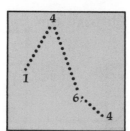

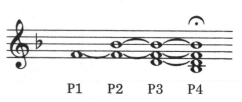

Check yourself with the bells.
Score points as before.

DAY IS DONE (TAPS)

Traditional

Tune Up:

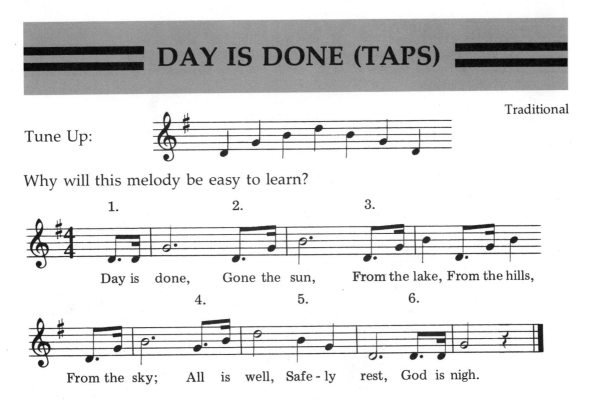

Why will this melody be easy to learn?

1. Day is done,
2. Gone the sun,
3. From the lake, From the hills,
4. From the sky;
5. All is well, Safe-ly
6. rest, God is nigh.

Sing it in a special way. Divide into six groups.
Each group sings one pattern.
Sustain your last tone so that all groups sound together.
"Catch" a breath when you need it, but keep the sound going!

GLORIA

Make up your own "Gloria." Divide into three groups.
Each group sings and sustains one syllable of the word "Gloria."
Sing using the chord sequence I, IV, V7, I.

		6 a---			
Group 1	5 a---			5 a---	5 a---
		4 ri----			
Group 2	3 ri----				3 ri----
			2 ri----		
Group 3	1 glo------	1 glo------			1 glo------
			7, glo------		

Choose a conductor to indicate when each group is to start and stop.
The conductor should also indicate **dynamics, articulations,** and **tempos.**

ADD YOUR OWN ACCOMPANIMENT

If the **I** chord uses these scale steps,

5
3
1

the **IV** chord uses these scale steps,

1'
6
4

and the **V7** chord uses these scale steps,

4'
2'
7
5

then can you decide when each chord should be used to accompany "Oleana"? Name the chord you will use in each measure.

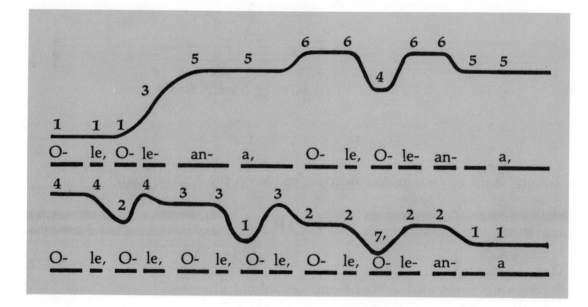

Look at the notation for "Oleana" on the next page.
A harmonizing part is given. Study its notation.
Why will the harmonizing part sound right with the melody?

OLEANA

English Words by Beth Landis

Norwegian Folk Song
Arranged by Kurt Miller

Refrain

O - le, O - le,   O - le, O - le,

(Melody)

O - le, O - le - an - a,   O - le, O - le - an - a,

Fine

O - le, O - le, O - le, O - le - an - a.

O - le, O - le, O - le, O - le, O - le, O - le - an - a.

Verse

1. O that is where I'd like to be, There where the land is free;
2. The hens lay eggs as big as rocks, Roost-ers crow like eight-day clocks,
3. The sal - mon leap so high up there, Hold your ket - tle in the air;
4. O come and bring your fid - dle, Dance to the mid - dle,

D.C. al Fine

Wheat and corn they grow so high, The tas - sels dust-ing off the sky!
Roast-ed pigs run all a - bout With knives and forks stuck in their snouts!
They'll jump in, pull on the lid, And cook them-selves to look like squid!
O - le with his vi - o - lin Will help us make a mer - ry din!

SWEET POTATOES

Adapted and Arranged by Jean La Coste

Creole Folk Song

Accompaniments:

Medium Drum

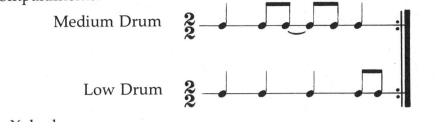

Low Drum

Bass Xylophone

Alto Xylophone, Part 1

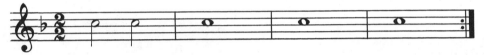

Alto Xylophone, Part 2

Use two mallets in playing the alto xylophone parts.
Strike mallets on the bars rapidly to create a "marimba roll" sound.

GRAND WALKAROUND
from *Cakewalk Suite*

Adapted by Hershey Kay
from Louis Moreau Gottschalk

This music is based in part on the song you have just learned.
Listen as the first melody returns again and again.

OLIVER

Words and Music
by Lionel Bart

Food, Glorious Food

Food, glorious food! Hot sausage and mustard!
While we're in the mood, cold jelly and custard!
Pease pudding and saveloys! "What next?" is the question.
Rich gentlemen have it; boys, "Indygestion"!

Where Is Love?

Where is love? Does it fall from skies above?
Is it underneath the willow tree that I've been dreaming of?
Where, where, is love?

Consider Yourself

Consider yourself one of us!

I'd Do Anything for You

I'd do anything for you, dear, anything.
For you mean ev'rything to me.

Would you lace my shoe? Anything!
Paint your face bright blue? Anything!

I'd risk ev'rything for one kiss, ev'rything;
Yes, I'd do anything, anything for you.

Who Will Buy?

Who will buy this wonderful feeling?
I'm so high, I swear I could fly.
Me, oh my! I don't want to lose it,
So what am I to do, to keep the sky so blue?
There must be someone who will buy.

CIRCLE PLAY

Play   ● = silence

●	●	●	4	●	●	●	●	●	●	●	●
1	2	3	4	5	6	7	8	9	10	11	12

Feel the beat

1	2	3	4	5	6	7	●	9	●	11	12
1	2	3	4	5	6	7	8	9	10	11	12

1	●	●	●	●	●	7	●	●	●	●	●
1	2	3	4	5	6	7	8	9	10	11	12

1	2	3	4	5	6	7	8	9	10	11	12
1	2	3	4	5	6	7	8	9	10	11	12

1	2	●	●	●	●	7	8	●	●	●	●
1	2	3	4	5	6	7	8	9	10	11	12

1	2	●	●	5	6	●	●	9	10	●	●
1	2	3	4	5	6	7	8	9	10	11	12

Improvise											
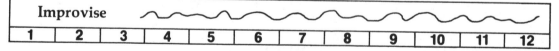
1	2	3	4	5	6	7	8	9	10	11	12

FORWARD—BACK!

Drummer: plays drum 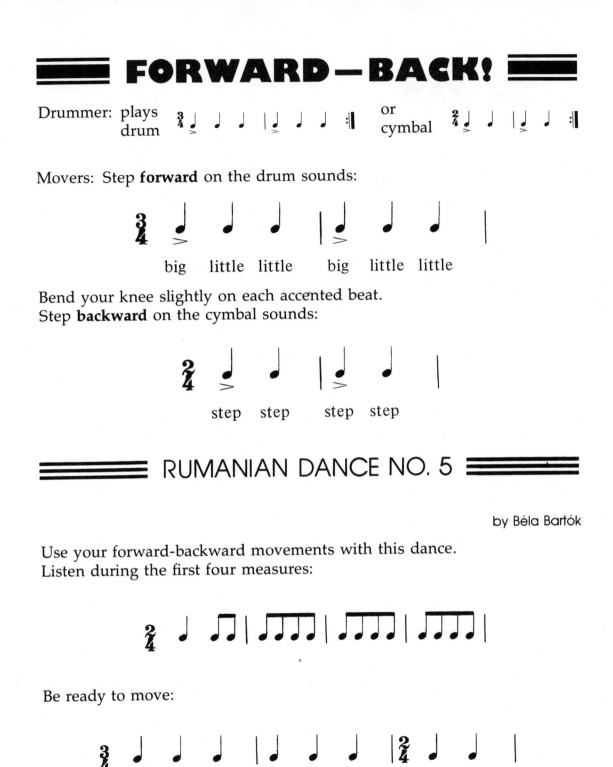 or cymbal

Movers: Step **forward** on the drum sounds:

big   little   little   big   little   little

Bend your knee slightly on each accented beat.
Step **backward** on the cymbal sounds:

step   step   step   step

RUMANIAN DANCE NO. 5

by Béla Bartók

Use your forward-backward movements with this dance.
Listen during the first four measures:

Be ready to move:

Can you describe the changes in meter for the entire dance?

COME, COME, YE SAINTS

"All Is Well"

Words by William Clayton

Adapted from T. J. White

Set an *andante* tempo.

When the meter is
in 4/4, walk forward:

Continue the stepping pattern as you sing "Come, Come Ye Saints."

1. Come, come, ye saints, no toil nor la - bor fear,
2. We'll find the place which God for us pre- pared

But with joy wend our way.
Far a - way in the West,

Though hard to you this jour - ney may ap - pear,
Where none shall come to hurt or make a - fraid;

Grace shall be as your day.
There the saints will be blessed.

'Tis ___ bet - ter far ___ for us to strive, ___
We'll ___ make the air ___ with mu - sic ring, ___

Our use - less cares ___ from us to drive;
Shout prais - es to ___ our God and King;

Do this, and joy your hearts will swell,
A - bove the rest these words we'll tell,

All is well! all is well!
All is well! all is well!

YANKEE DOODLE BOY

Words and Music by George M. Cohan

I'm a Yan - kee Doo - dle Dan - dy,

A Yan - kee Doo - dle, do or die;

A real live neph - ew of my Un - cle Sam,

Born on the Fourth of Ju - ly.

I've got a Yan - kee Doo - dle sweet - heart,

She's my Yan - kee Doo - dle joy.

Yan - kee Doo - dle came to Lon - don, just to ride the po - nies,

I am a Yan - kee Doo - dle boy._____

≡ **Patriotic Polyrhythms** ≡

Clap the rhythm pattern of the words for these two songs:

"America"   "America, the Beautiful"

Form two groups. Clap the patterns of both songs at the same time.

Be sure to accent the first beat in each measure.

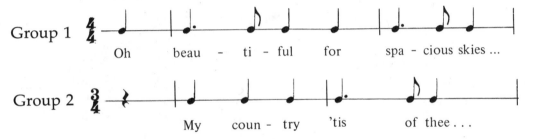

Group 1   Oh   beau – ti – ful   for   spa - cious skies ...

Group 2   My   coun - try   'tis   of thee ...

How do the rhythm patterns compare with each other?

Do the accents fall on the same beat for both songs?

Do the songs end at different times? same time?

Perform again using two different timbres, such as sticks and drums.

What effect does the use of two different timbres have on
the performance?

Flag, 1958, Jasper Johns. Collection of Mr. and Mrs. Leo Castelli.

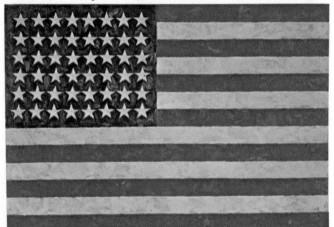

PUTNAM'S CAMP, REDDING, CONNECTICUT

from *Three Places in New England*

by Charles Ives

Follow the call numbers as you listen to this musical description
of a boy's Fourth of July celebration in the late nineteenth century.
Can you hear the tunes in the Music Map as each is played?

9.

10.

11.

marcato....sempre...marcato

12.

CHECK YOUR MUSICAL STRENGTH (4)

Can you:
- perform polytonal melodies as a member of a group?
- perform polyrhythms as a member of a group?
- perform music using mixed meters as a member of a group?
- arrange a song to be sung in harmony?

Explore the following ideas for making music.
After each experience, decide whether you
used polytonality, polyrhythms, or mixed meters.

- Divide into two groups. One group may chant
  or clap the rhythm of "On Top of Old Smokey"
  (page 99), while another performs the
  rhythm of "Old Joe Clarke" (page 74).
- Compose two phrases of rhythm—one in threes,
  another in twos. Alternate playing the phrases without
  stopping in between. Use percussion instruments
  with contrasting tone qualities.
- Choose two members of the group to play a
  familiar melody, such as "Bingo"
  (page 82), on two sets of bells.
  One might play it in the key in which it is written.
  The other person might play it in C (begin on G).

SUNSHINE ON MY SHOULDERS

Words by John Denver

Music by John Denver,
Mike Taylor, and Dick Kniss

Rhythm of words

Shortest sounds

Steady beat

Sun-shine_ on my shoul-ders_ makes me hap-py,_

sun-shine_ in my eyes can make me cry._

G   C   G   C   G   C   G   C

Sun-shine__ on the wa-ter__ looks so love-ly,__

G   C   G   C   G   C   G   C

2nd time, skip to Coda

sun-shine__ al-most al-ways__ makes me high._____

G   Am7   Bm   C   G   Am7

If I had a day   that I could give you,__
If I had a tale   that I could tell you,__

Bm   C   G   Am7   Bm   C   3

I'd give to you__ a day   just like to-
I'd tell a tale__ sure   to make you

Am7   D7   G   Am7

day._____ If I had__ a
smile._____ If I had__ a

119

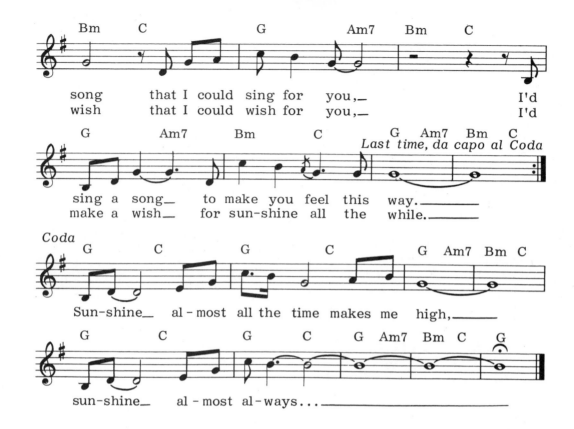

song   that I could sing for   you,___   I'd
wish   that I could wish for   you,___   I'd

Last time, da capo al Coda

sing a song___   to make you feel this   way._____
make a wish___   for sun-shine all   the   while._____

Coda

Sun-shine___ al-most all the time makes me   high,_____

sun-shine___ al-most al-ways..._____

Play the following bass xylophone and alto metallophone parts
as a repeated accompaniment for the first four lines of the song.

Bass Xylophone

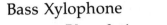

Alto Metallophone

Add these special glockenspiel parts to your arrangement.
Use them to perform an introduction, interlude, or coda.

Soprano Glockenspiel

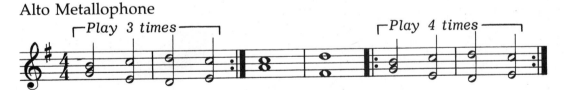

Alto Glockenspiel

MORE MUSIC TO EXPLORE

Perform by Singing and Playing

═══ MUSIC ALONE SHALL LIVE ═══

German Round

Perform this music in an ensemble.
- Sing the melody expressively.
- Sing it as a round.
- Add the sounds of instruments.
- Can you listen to the other parts as you perform your own?

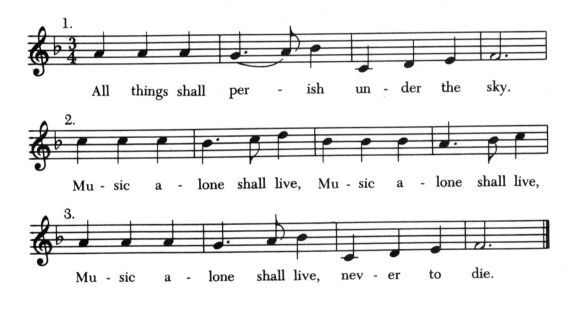

1. All things shall per - ish un - der the sky.

2. Mu - sic a - lone shall live, Mu - sic a - lone shall live,

3. Mu - sic a - lone shall live, nev - er to die.

Soprano Glockenspiel or Bells

Bass Xylophone or Piano

F   C   C   F

123

SING

Words and Music
by Joe Raposo

Moderately

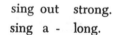

1. Sing!   Sing a   song.   Sing out loud,
2. Sing!   Sing a   song.   Let the world

sing out strong.   Sing of good things, not
sing a - long.   Sing the love there could

bad;   Sing of hap - py, not sad.
be --   Sing for you and for me.

Sing!   Sing a   song.   Make it sim - ple to

last your whole life long. _____   Don't wor - ry that it's not

good e - nough for an-y-one else to hear. Sing!

Sing a song! ____ La la do la da, La

da la do la da, La da da la do la la. ____

La do la da, La da la la da, Lo da da la do lo da. __

repeat and fade

____ ____ La la do la da, La

da la do la da, La da da la do la da. __

PRETTY PEÑA

Words by Eunice Boardman

Mexican Folk Melody

Listen to voices singing

in unison

in thirds

Show when you hear voices singing

in unison

in thirds

1. Soft - ly, a voice is sing - ing; Gent - ly, its mes - sage
2. Come now, O pret - ty Pe - ña; Hur - ry, it is Fi -

bring - ing. Pe - ña, come to your win - dow! The sounds of
es - ta! Lis - ten, the hap - py tam-bour-ines Are call - ing

ser - e - nad - ing fill the sum - mer air! ____ } Gui - tars are
us to join the danc - ers in the square! __ }

play - ing, their mu - sic say - ing; Come pret - ty

Pe - ña! No more de - lay - ing!
Whirl - ing, the danc - ers

Hur - ry! Come to your

win - dow, The sounds of ser - e - nad - ing fill the sum - mer air!
swirl - ing, Are call - ing us to gay Fi - es - ta in the square!

Sing in unison

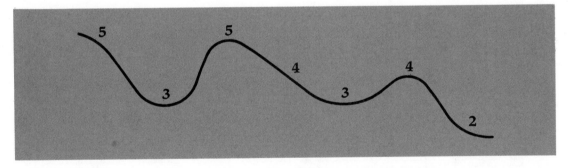

and in thirds.

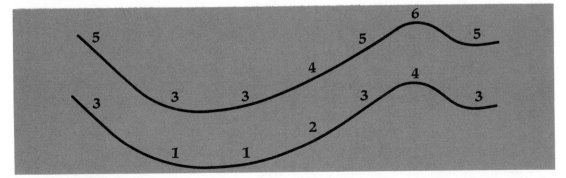

SO LONG

Words and Music
by Woody Guthrie

Show when you hear
unison

thirds

When will you show pitches that are farther apart?
sixths

1. I've sung this song but I'll sing it a - gain,
2. A dust storm hit and it hit ____ like thun-der,
3. We talked of the end of the world, __ and then

Of the place where I lived on the wild wind - y plains,
It ___ dust - ed us o - ver and cov - ered us un - der,
We'd __ sing ____ a song and then sing it a - gain,

In the month called A - pril, the coun - ty called Gray,
It ___ blocked out the traf - fic and blocked out the sun,
We'd __ sit for an hour ____ and not say a word,

And here's what all of the peo-ple there say:
And straight for home all the peo-ple did run, sing-ing:
And then this tune and these words would be heard:

Refrain

"So long, it's been good to know you,

So long, it's been good to know you,

So long, it's been good to know you,

This dust-y old dust is a-get-ting my home,

I've got to be mov-ing a-long."_____

On which words of the song do you hear the interval of a sixth?
Perform this song singing in unison, thirds, and sixths.

SOUND PAIRS

How well do you hear intervals?
Play a game.
Walk around the room in pairs, moving to a steady beat.
Listen to the musician.
Show what you hear.

Movers   Musician

Unison

Play one pitch.

Thirds

Play two pitches at
the same time, three
steps apart.

Sixths

Play two pitches at
the same time, six
steps apart.

DUST OF SNOW

Words by Robert Frost

Music by Arthur Frackenpohl

Tune Up:

As you sing this melody in unison, thirds, and sixths, you will also need to sing two new intervals. Can you find them? Show the distance between voices as you sing.

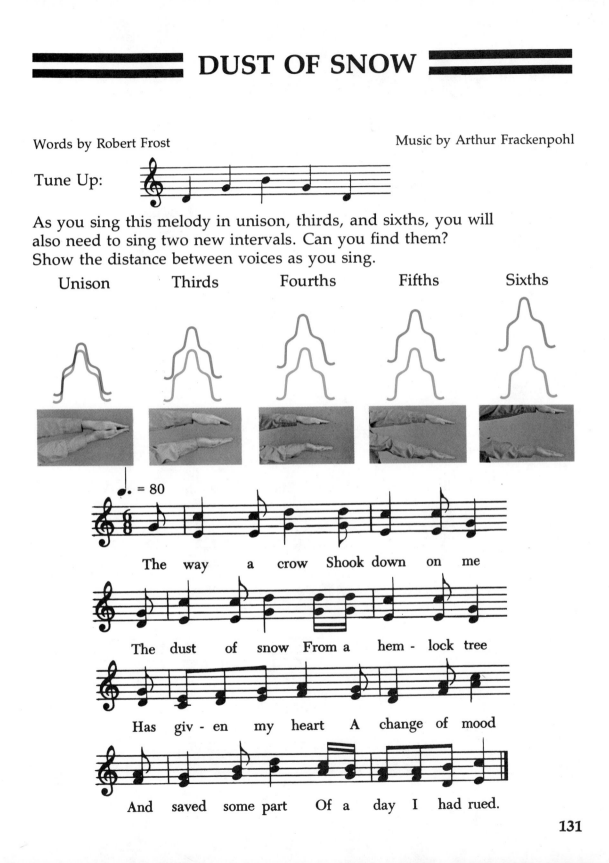

Unison   Thirds   Fourths   Fifths   Sixths

The way a crow Shook down on me

The dust of snow From a hem - lock tree

Has giv - en my heart A change of mood

And saved some part Of a day I had rued.

THE CARAVAN

English Words Adapted

Arabian Folk Song

Add your own harmonizing part.

When you see [staff], sing in unison: [staff]

When you see [staff] or [staff], sing in thirds: [staff]

When you see [staff], sing a sixth: [staff]

On the des - ert, pa - tient cam - els la - den with spi - ces and

gold,   Tread - ing   soft - ly   on   deep   car - pets of

sand   just as   in   days of   old.   Li - li - li - li - li   the

driv - ers sing.   Ding - a - ling - a - ling the cam - el bells ring.

132

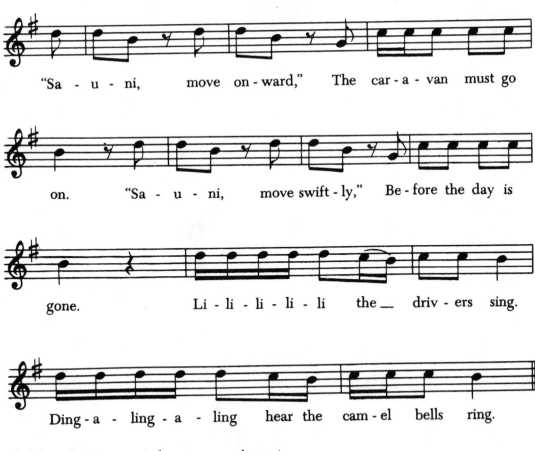

"Sa - u - ni, move on - ward," The car - a - van must go on. "Sa - u - ni, move swift - ly," Be - fore the day is gone. Li - li - li - li - li the __ driv - ers sing. Ding - a - ling - a - ling hear the cam - el bells ring.

Add an instrumental accompaniment.

Use tambourine or finger cymbals:

Play this pattern on piano, cello, or bass xylophone:

G D G   G D G

133

DEEP IN THE HEART OF TEXAS

Words by June Hershey

Music by Don Swander

Show what you hear!

V7

I

Sing what you hear!
    Verse: Sing in unison.
    Refrain: Some may sing the **chord roots.**
      What pitches will you sing?

There is a land, a west-ern land, Might-y

won-der-ful to see ____ It is the land I

un-der-stand, And it's there I long to be. ____

Refrain

The stars at night are big and bright, Deep in the

heart of Tex - as! _____ The prai - rie sky is

wide and high, Deep in the heart of Tex-as! _____ The

sage in bloom is like per - fume, Deep in the heart of

Tex - as! _____ Re - minds me of the one I

love, Deep in the heart of Tex - as! _____

Create a harmony part for "Old Joe Clarke" (page 74)
by adding a root bass. Use two pitches, F and C.

MAGIC PENNY

Words and Music
by Malvina Reynolds

Use what you have learned about part singing
to harmonize this song.
Sing root basses in the first section:

Eb

Love   is   some - thing if you give it   a - way,—

Bb7   Eb

Give   it   a - way,—   give   it   a - way,—

Eb   Eb

Love   is   some - thing if you give it   a - way.

Bb7   Eb   *Fine*

You   end   up   hav - ing   more.

136

Sing a third below:

It's just like a mag - ic pen - ny.

Hold it tight and you won't have an - y;

Lend it; spend_ it, and you'll have so man - y

Sing in unison:

they'll roll all o - ver the floor, for

D.C. al fine

137

MORE SOUND PAIRS

Movers | Musicians

Seconds

Play pitches side by side.

Fourths

Play two pitches, four steps apart.

Fifths

Play two pitches, five steps apart.

Octaves

Play two pitches, eight steps apart.

Which of the Sound Pair Combination games can you play successfully?

Game 1: unisons, thirds, sixths
Game 2: seconds, fifths, octaves
Game 3: unisons, fourths, sixths
Game 4: any of the intervals

CHOPSTICKS

Make up new words to this familiar tune.
The harmony uses intervals of a
      second   third   fourth   sixth   octave
Try singing your own words in two-part harmony.
One group reads and sings the top notes;
the other reads and sings the bottom notes.

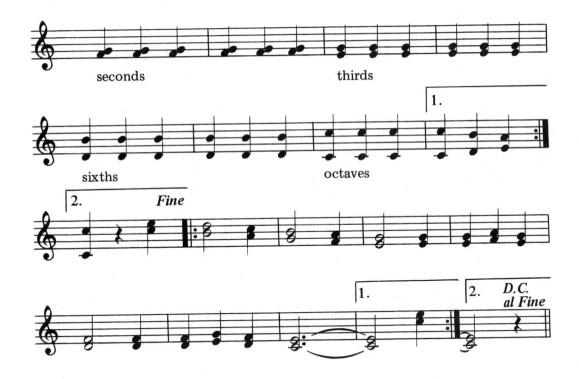

SOMEBODY'S KNOCKIN' AT YOUR DOOR

Spiritual
Arranged by Buryl A. Red

Sing a harmonizing part by echoing the melody.
When is the harmonizing part no longer an echo?

Some-bod - y's knock-ing at your door, _____

Some-bod - y's knock-ing at your

Some-bod - y's knock-ing at your door; _____

door, _____ Some-bod - y's knock-ing at your

O _____ sin - ner, why don't you an - swer?

door; O sin - ner, why don't you an - swer? Some-bod - y's

THE COLORADO TRAIL

Cowboy Song
Arranged by Kurt Miller

Add a harmonizing part by singing a contrasting melody.

oo _____ oo _____

(Melody)

Eyes like the morn- ing star, Cheek like a rose,

oo _____ oo _____

Lau - ra was a pret- ty girl, ev - ery-bod - y knows.

oo _____ oo _____

Weep, all ye lit - tle rains, Wail, winds, ___ wail,

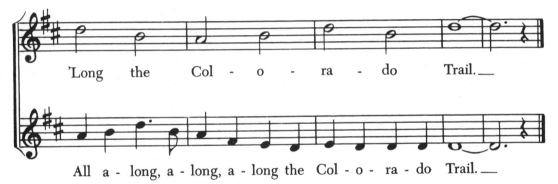

'Long the Col - o - ra - do Trail. __

All a - long, a - long, a - long the Col - o - ra - do Trail. __

Listen to this contrasting melody on the recording.
Can someone learn to play it on bells or violin?

rubato

THE INCH WORM

Words and Music by Frank Loesser

Slowly

Two and two are four, four and four are eight;

That's all you have on your busi - ness - like mind.

Two and two are four, four and four are eight;

How can you be so blind?_____

Refrain

Two and two are four, Four and four are eight,

Inch worm, inch worm, mea - sur - ing the mar - i - golds,

Eight and eight are six - teen, Six - teen and six - teen are thir - ty two.

You and your a - rith - me - tic, you'll prob - a - bly go far._____

Two and two are four, Four and four are eight,

Inch worm, inch worm, mea-sur-ing the mar-i-golds,

Eight and eight are six - teen, Six - teen and six-teen are thir-ty two.

Seems to me you'd stop and see how beau-ti-ful they are.

Use a low-pitched instrument. Play this bass pattern as an accompaniment for the refrain.

1.   2.

C   Bb   A   G   F   Eb   D   Db   C   C   C   F

Improvise a melodic interlude that "sounds good" with the bass pattern. Use only these three pitches:

STEAL AWAY

Spiritual

This arrangement adds harmonizing parts in several ways.
Find places where voices move in thirds, sixths, or other intervals.
Are there any echo parts?
Are there places where the second part is a contrasting melody?

146

THE MUSICIAN AT WORK...
IN RADIO AND TELEVISION

You might be a

Disc Jockey

You would need to:
- know current recordings.
- be aware of the current "pop scene."
- select appealing recordings for broadcast.
- research and present interesting information about recording artists.

Classical Music Commentator

You would need to:
- know about performers, composers, and many styles of music.
- select an interesting variety of music for broadcast.
- pronounce foreign names and terms.
- interview performing artists.

Composer

You would need to:
- write jingles for commercials.
- write background and title music for programs.
- know the possibilities and limitations of instruments and voices.
- orchestrate music for various combinations of instruments.

Singer

You would need to:
- have special skills in singing.
- have skill in sightsinging.
- memorize quickly.
- dance, as well as sing, for musical shows.

Sound Engineer

You would need to:
- operate complex audiovisual equipment.
- make decisions about balancing sound levels, and mixing and blending instruments and voices.

Instrumentalist

You would need to:
- have special skill in playing one or more instruments.
- read music fluently.
- transpose music into other keys.
- improvise music.
- be skillful in ensemble playing.

HEAR–MAKE–PLAY– FOLK INSTRUMENTS

People came to this country in the early days bringing
instruments from their native lands. They added sounds by
making their own instruments out of materials they could easily find.
Listen to the accompaniment of "Sourwood Mountain."
Which of the instruments shown on these pages can you hear?

SOURWOOD MOUNTAIN

Kentucky Folk Song

Chick - en crow-in' on Sour - wood Moun-tain,
So man - y pret - ty girls, I can't count 'em,

Hey de - ing dang did - dle al - ly day.
Hey de - ing dang did - dle al - ly day.

My true love, she lives in Letch - er,
She won't come and I won't fetch her,

Hey de - ing dang did - dle al - ly day.
Hey de - ing dang did - dle al - ly day.

BIRD IN THE TREE

Irish Folk Song

Listen to this special type of violin playing known as "fiddling."
Can you identify how it is different from other ways of playing violin?

BIG BEN

Traditional

"Big Ben" is in the style known as bluegrass music.
Which of these instruments takes the "lead"?

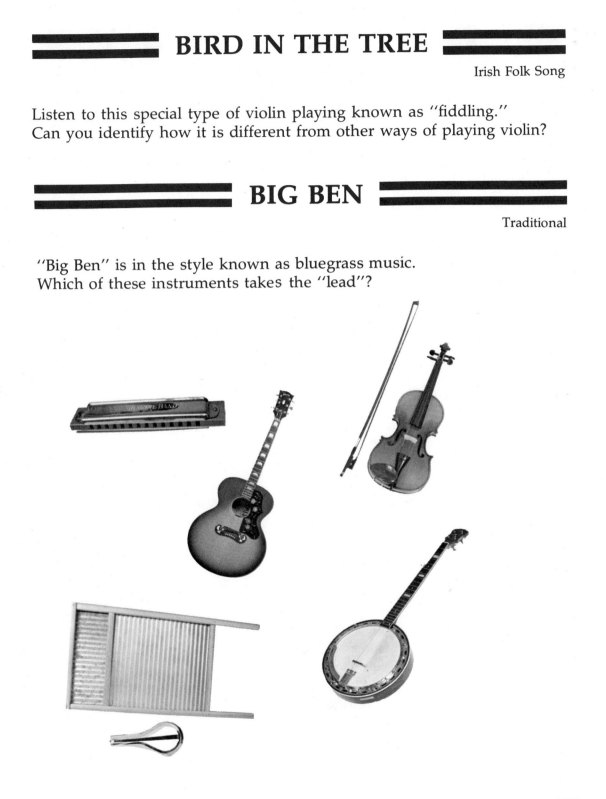

MAKE YOUR OWN FOLK INSTRUMENTS
A One-String Dulcimer

Materials
1. One 1" by 2" board, about 33" long.
2. One ⅜" screw eye (**tuning peg**) and one ½" nail·
3. An ice cream stick, split in two pieces lengthwise (**nut** and **bridge**).
4. One guitar or banjo string.

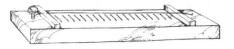

Tools

You will need a hammer, pocket knife, coping saw, and staple gun with ³/₁₆" staples.

To Make
1. Prepare the board by sanding as smooth as possible.
2. Put in **frets.** Set in the staples following the marks so that they will lie under the string.

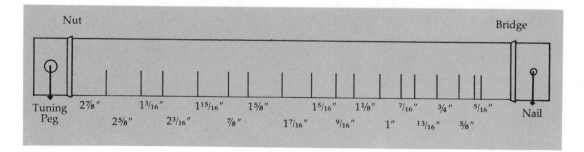

3. Glue the **nut** to the board on edge.
4. Put in the **tuning peg** just deep enough to hold.
5. Hammer the nail into the bridge end of the dulcimer.
6. String the dulcimer.
7. Set the bridge on edge under the string.
8. Turn the screw eye to tune the instrument.

Play Your
One-String Dulcimer

You need: ● a **noter,** made from a small round stick
  ● a **pick,** cut from a plastic milk bottle
The third fret will be the **tonal center,** or **1.**

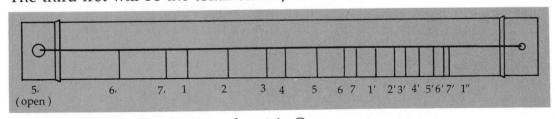

5,   6,   7,   1   2   3   4   5   6 7   1' 2'3' 4' 5'6'7' 1"
(open)

Try to tune your dulcimer so that **1** is C.
Hold the **pick** in your **right hand.**
Pluck the string by moving your hand back toward yourself.

Hold the **noter** in your **left hand.** Move it higher and lower, pressing down just behind each fret to change pitches.

Can you play "Skip to My Lou," following the diagram to move back and forth along the dulcimer?

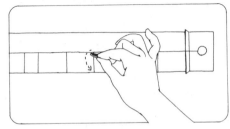

SKIP TO MY LOU

Move the noter back and forth. Pluck the rhythm with the pick.

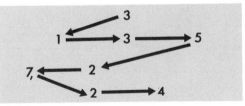

Can you finish the tune?

Listen to this folk medley. It is performed on guitar and dulcimer.
After listening to the recording, decide what the word **medley** means.

What familiar songs do you recognize?

FAREWELL MY OWN TRUE LOVE

American Folk Song
Collected by William S. Haynie

Lonesome ballads such as these are often played on the dulcimer
or accompanied while the performer sings.

Try adding this accompaniment on your one-string dulcimer.
If your dulcimer is tuned to C, start on the F fret (fourth above C).

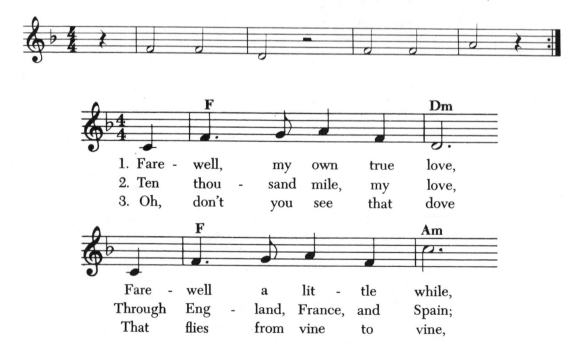

1. Fare - well,   my   own   true   love,
2. Ten   thou - sand mile, my   love,
3. Oh,   don't   you   see   that   dove

Fare - well   a   lit - tle   while,
Through Eng - land, France, and   Spain;
That   flies   from vine   to   vine,

I'm goin' a - way but I'll come a - gain,
My rov - ing mind shall — nev - er rest
A - mourn - ing for his — own true love,

If I go ten thou - sand mile.
Till I see your face a - gain.
Just as I will mourn for mine.

MAKE A "DEVIL'S DREAM"

This instrument can be made from any sound source the inventor can find. Follow the instructions to make a **Devil's Dream** just like this one, or invent your own.

Materials
1. a rake or broom handle
2. a 2' length of lathe
3. an ice cream stick
4. a 5" or 6" pot lid (take off knob)
5. a small tambourine
6. a 5-string banjo bridge and a #4 banjo string
7. a violin tuning peg
8. a metal kazoo and a cowbell, or any other noise gadgets!

To Make
1. Drill a hole near the top of the rake handle for a tuning peg. Insert the tuning peg.
2. Fasten the tambourine near the bottom of the rake handle.
3. Put a tiny nail into the lower edge of the tambourine.
4. Glue the ice cream stick just below the tuning peg.
5. Fasten the string to the tuning peg and the nail in the tambourine.
6. Fasten the pot lid cymbal to the top of the handle.
7. Fasten a piece of lathe a little below the tuning peg on the back of the pole. Fasten the kazoo to it.
8. Add any other sound makers you wish.

156

Play Your Devil's Dream

Melody
Sing a song or hum into the kazoo to produce
a melody while you play on the Devil's Dream.

Playing Percussion
Accompany the melody by playing rhythm ideas
on the various percussion instruments
attached to the Devil's Dream.
Tie a mallet or beater on your wrist so that
you will be able to play percussion
instruments.

Playing String
Play melody or root bass on the string of
the Devil's Dream.
Hold one finger of your left hand down
on the string with the rest of the hand
behind the neck.
Now pick the string with your right hand.
If you slide your left hand up and down
the string, the notes will change from
higher to lower.

1. Try picking out a simple tune.
2. Play a two-tone root bass accompaniment
   for "Skip to My Lou."
3. Play "Old Joe Clarke."

HOP UP, MY LADIES

American Folk Song

Listen to the recording. The accompaniment is played on
popular folk instruments. Notice how the melody is passed from
harmonica to banjo to fiddle.

1. Did you ev - er go to meet - ing, Un - cle Joe, Un - cle Joe?
2. Will your horse __ car - ry dou - ble, Un - cle Joe, Un - cle Joe?
3. Is your horse a sin - gle foot - er, Un - cle Joe, Un - cle Joe?

Did you ev - er go to meet - ing, Un - cle Joe? __
Will your horse __ car - ry dou - ble, Un - cle Joe? __
Is your horse a sin - gle foot - er, Un - cle Joe? __

Did you ev - er go to meet - ing, Un - cle Joe, Un - cle Joe?
Will your horse __ car - ry dou - ble, Un - cle Joe, Un - cle Joe?
Is your horse a sin - gle foot - er, Un - cle Joe, Un - cle Joe?

Don't mind the weath - er, so the winds don't blow.
Don't mind the weath - er, so the winds don't blow.
Don't mind the weath - er, so the winds don't blow.

Refrain

Hop up, my la - dies, three in a row,

158

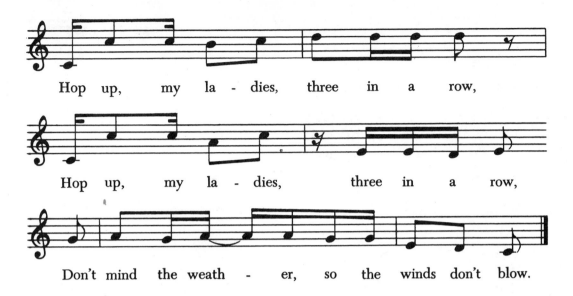

Hop up, my la - dies, three in a row,

Hop up, my la - dies, three in a row,

Don't mind the weath - er, so the winds don't blow.

4. Would you rather own a pacer, Uncle Joe, Uncle Joe?
   Don't mind the weather, so the winds don't blow. *Refrain.*

5. Say, you don't want to gallop, Uncle Joe, Uncle Joe.
   Don't mind the weather, so the winds don't blow. *Refrain*

6. Say, you might take a tumble, Uncle Joe, Uncle Joe.
   Don't mind the weather, so the winds don't blow. *Refrain*

7. Well, we'll get there soon as the others, Uncle Joe.
   Don't mind the weather, so the winds don't blow. *Refrain*

YACKETY SAX

Music by Randy Randolph and James Rich

Learn an American **novelty dance.**
The instrument featured in this music is an alto saxophone.
First, listen to the music as you follow this guide.

Introduction
Main theme, saxophone
Main theme repeated, saxophone
Interlude
Main theme varied, trumpet
Main theme varied, saxophone
Interlude
Original main theme, saxophone
Coda

Choose a partner and form a circle.
The circle will move in a clockwise direction.
Read and practice the movements.
Select a caller to tell you how and when to move as the
music is played.

Music	Caller
Introduction	Everybody clap four times!
Main theme	Left heel point, left heel point,
	Vine to the left.
	Right heel point, right heel point,
	Vine to the right.
	Two steps forward, four times.
	Leave your partner, back 'round you go.
Interlude	Everybody clap four times.

Perform the complete dance.
When the melody is varied, can you vary the dance?

≡ PLAY THE AUTOHARP ≡

 How to play:
Learn the basics.

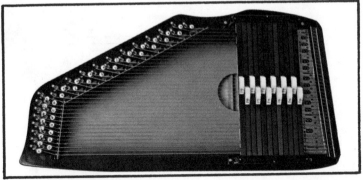

1 Strum with right hand crossed over left. Use a pick.

2 Press chord buttons firmly with fingers of left hand.

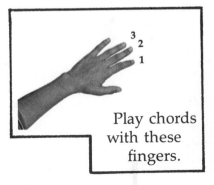

Play chords with these fingers.

Try different strums:

all strings: up stroke (away from body)

down stroke (toward body)

some strings: low ——— middle —✗— high ———

B When to play:
Try a simple strum.
Begin by playing only on the accented beats.
F = I, B♭ = IV, C7 = V7

Begin melody on F.

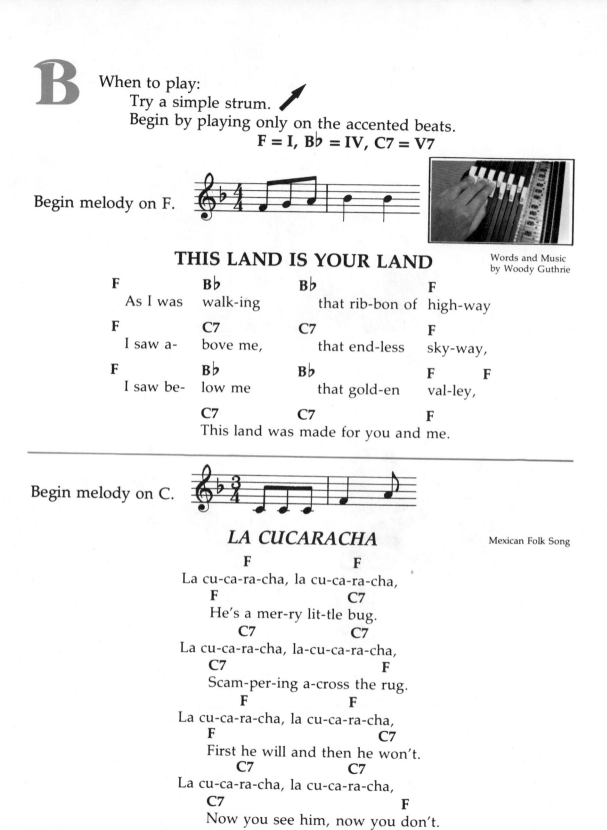

THIS LAND IS YOUR LAND

Words and Music
by Woody Guthrie

F	B♭	B♭	F
As I was	walk-ing	that rib-bon of	high-way

F	C7	C7	F
I saw a-	bove me,	that end-less	sky-way,

F	B♭	B♭	F	F
I saw be-	low me	that gold-en	val-ley,	

C7	C7	F
This land was made for you and me.		

Begin melody on C.

LA CUCARACHA

Mexican Folk Song

     F   **F**
La cu-ca-ra-cha, la cu-ca-ra-cha,
     F   **C7**
He's a mer-ry lit-tle bug.
     C7   **C7**
La cu-ca-ra-cha, la-cu-ca-ra-cha,
     C7   **F**
Scam-per-ing a-cross the rug.
     F   **F**
La cu-ca-ra-cha, la cu-ca-ra-cha,
     F   **C7**
First he will and then he won't.
     C7   **C7**
La cu-ca-ra-cha, la cu-ca-ra-cha,
     C7   **F**
Now you see him, now you don't.

C Try some other strums.

Strums to use with:

"This Land Is Your Land"

"La Cucaracha"

Here are some "finger pickin'" patterns.
Use thumb and finger picks.

T = thumb
I = index finger
M = middle finger

OH SUSANNAH

Words and Music
by Stephen Foster

1. I___ came from Al - a - bam - a, With my
2. It___ rained all night the day I left, The

ban - jo on my knee, I'm___ going to Loui - si -
weath - er it was dry, The___ sun so hot I

an - a, There my true love for to see;
froze to death, Su -san - na, don't you cry.

Refrain

Oh! Su - san - na, Oh, don't you cry for me, I've___

come from Al - a - bam - a With my ban - jo on my knee.

D Create special effects.

ROCK ISLAND LINE

Work Song

With a steady beat

I say the Rock Is land Line ___ is a might-y good road, ___ I say the Rock Is - land Line ___ is the road to ride; Oh, the Rock Is - land Line ___ is a might-y good road, ___ If you want to ride it, got to ride it like you're fly - in'; Buy your tick - et at the sta - tion on the Rock Is - land Line.

Form your hand in a loose fist.
Make a special train effect.
Strum only on lowest strings.

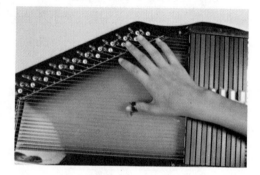

Look through your music book.
Choose songs you like.
Plan your own strum.

164

Talkin' Blues

Develop a dialogue with your autoharp.

"Talk" the blues in the rhythm notated below as you accompany yourself with different strums on the autoharp.

Create an interlude at the end of each phrase.

Try to make the autoharp "answer" you by imitating the rhythm and pitch inflection of your voice.

If you want to get to hea - ven let me tell you what to do,

Got - ta grease your feet in mut- ton stew,

Slide right out of the slip - p'ry sand and

ooze ov - er in the prom - ised land.

Add your own "Talkin' Blues." Try beginning with this line:
"If you want to get to hea-ven, bet-ter start out right, . . ."

Pick a tune.
Use a "pinching motion"; strum up with your
thumb and, at the same time, down with your fingers.

Strum once for each note in the melody.
To help, you may want to mark the tune's lowest and highest
pitches on the autoharp.
Tie a thread to these two strings.
Don't worry about locating the exact pitch. Just get "in the
vicinity" of the string and it will sound all right!

SKIP TO MY LOU

Eb(I)   Eb(I)

Choose your part - ner, skip to my Lou,

Bb7(V7)   Bb7(V7)

Choose your part - ner, skip to my Lou,

Eb(I)   Eb(I)

Choose your part - ner, skip to my Lou,

Ab(IV)   Bb7(V7)   Eb(I)

skip to my Lou, my dar - ling.

PLAY A KEYBOARD INSTRUMENT

Play using:
- one finger.
- several fingers, one after the other.
- many fingers; play a "handful" of sounds at one time.
- both hands; begin at one end, and go to the other, playing every black and white key.

Play

loud . . . soft

many sounds . . . few sounds

separate sounds . . . many sounds at one time

sounds that skip . . . sounds that move by steps

same sounds repeated again and again

slow . . . fast

long sounds . . . short sounds

Use these ideas to improvise a composition, as directed on the next page.

LOST IN ANOTHER WORLD

Work in pairs.
Use the sounds of the piano to express the ideas suggested.
Be sure each part of the sound story lasts long enough for
listeners to understand the idea you are expressing.

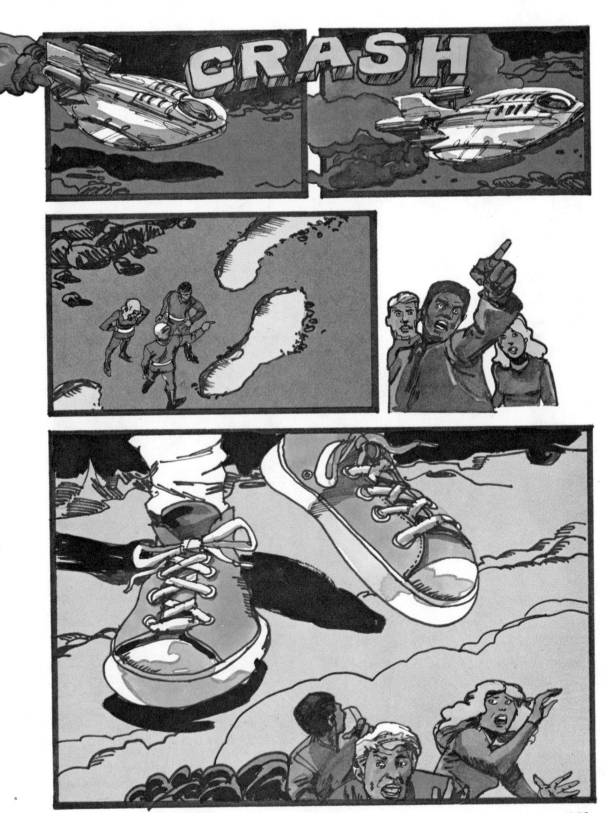

Perform your sound story. Ask class members to evaluate it.

KEYBOARD INSTRUMENTS

Can you identify which keyboard instruments you are hearing?

All of these instruments have keyboards.
Why don't they sound the same?

In what ways would the music of the pipe organ selection be different if performed on the harpsichord?

≡ Play on the Black Keys ≡

Find three black keys with
your right hand.
Move from one black key to
another by:

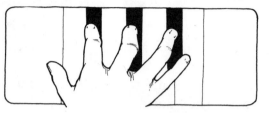

step: skip: repeat:

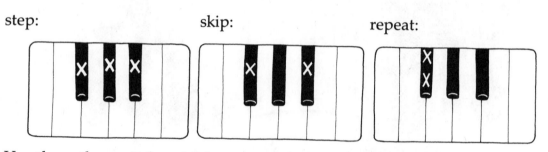

Use these three pitches. Make up a melody to fit this rhyme:

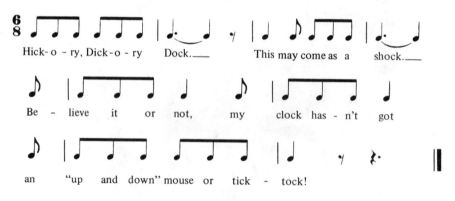

Hick- o - ry, Dick-o - ry Dock.___ This may come as a shock.___

Be - lieve it or not, my clock has - n't got

an "up and down" mouse or tick - tock!

Find two black keys next to the three you have already played.
Play them with your left hand.
Can you play "Old MacDonald"?

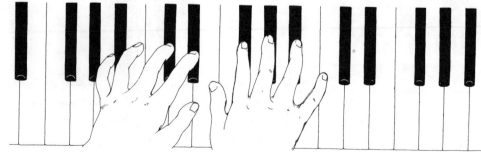

Play on the White Keys

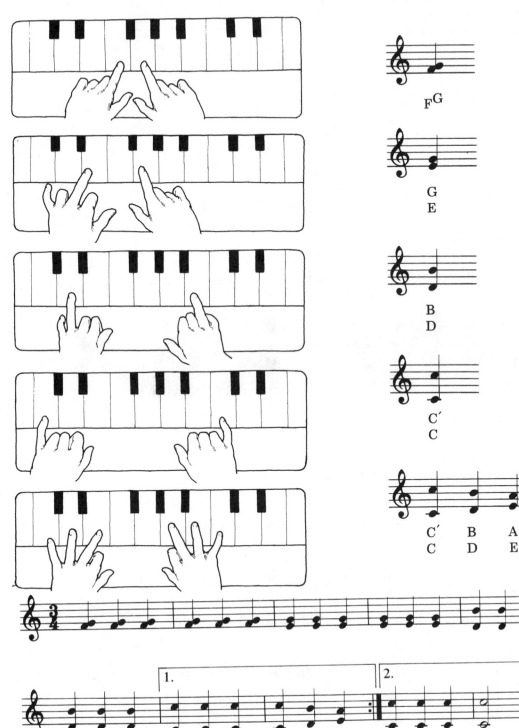

≡ Learn to Play a C Chord ≡

Play on the low part of
the keyboard.
Press the **root** of the chord
with the left index finger.
Play the other two tones of
the chord with the thumb and
middle finger of the right
hand.

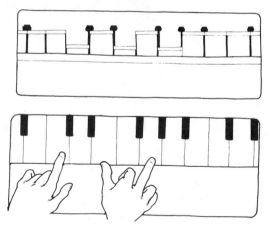

Use this chord to accompany a familiar song.
The beginning pitch for the song is C.

THREE BLIND MICE

Thrée blind míce, thrée blind míce,

Sée how they rún, sée how they rún;

They áll ran after the fármer's wife,

She cút off their tails with a cárving knife,

Did éver you see such a síght in your life

As thrée blind míce?

≡ Learn to Play a G⁷ Chord ≡

Change the finger positions from
the **C** chord to the **G7** chord.
Move the index finger of the
left hand from C to B.

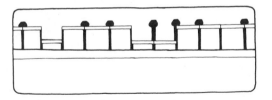

Leave the middle finger of the
right hand on G.

Use the index finger on F.
Remove the thumb from E.

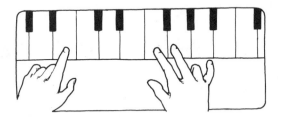

Practice moving back and forth between the chords several
times. Then accompany the following song.
Play on the first beat of each measure.

≡ POLLY WOLLY DOODLE ≡

American Folk Song

          C   C
Oh, I went down South to see my Sal,
          C   G7
Sing Polly wolly doodle all the day;
   G7   G7
My Sally is a spunky gal,
      G7   C
Sing Polly wolly doodle all the day.
            C   C
Fare thee well, fare thee well,
            C   G7
Fare thee well my fairy fay,
         G7   G7
For I'm going to Louisiana for to see my Susyanna,
   G7   C
Sing Polly wolly doodle all the day.

Return to the "Mystery Melody" on page 173.
Play these two chords as a new accompaniment for the melody.

175

Learn to Play an F Chord...

Play on the low part of the keyboard.

Press the root of the chord (F) with the left-hand index finger.

Play the remaining two tones of the chord with the thumb and middle finger of the right hand.

Use this chord to accompany a familiar song. The beginning pitch for the song is C.

IFCA'S CASTLE

Traditional Round

Above the pláin of góld and gréen

A yóung boy's héad is pláinly séen;

A hú-ya, hu-ya, hú-ya-ya, Swíftly flowing ríver,

A hú-ya, hu-ya, hú-ya-ya, Swíftly flowing ríver.

...and the C⁷ Chord

Move from the **F** chord
to the **C7** chord.
Practice moving back and forth
between the chords.
Accompany this song.

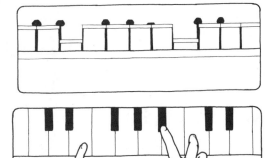

DOWN IN THE VALLEY

Kentucky Folk Song

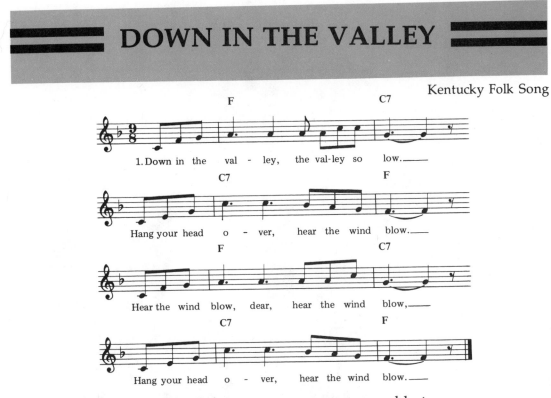

1. Down in the val-ley, the val-ley so low.___
Hang your head o - ver, hear the wind blow.___
Hear the wind blow, dear, hear the wind blow,___
Hang your head o - ver, hear the wind blow.___

Look through the book. Other songs you are now able to
accompany are:
"Sweet Potatoes" (page 104),
"Deep in the Heart of Texas" (page 136),
"Old Joe Clarke" (page 74).

Describe...
Create...

with words

with sounds

with gestures

with color, shape, line

DESCRIBE...
WHAT YOU SEE

Look at this painting.
Can you describe what you see: with words?
with movement?
with sound?

Tabago, Helen Frankenthaler.
Courtesy of Andre Emmerich Gallery, Private Collection. **179**

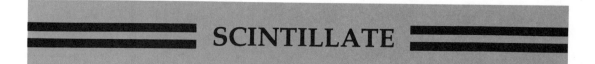

SCINTILLATE

Traditional

Look at this "musical score."
Can you describe how it will sound: with words?
with movement?
If you describe it well enough you should be able to name the original song.

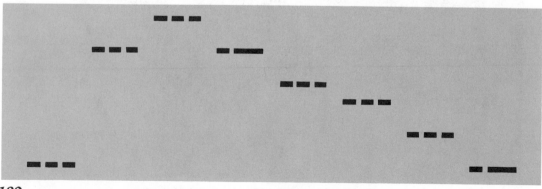

Could you figure out the title by describing how the rhythm
and melody would sound? If not, maybe the words will help!

> Scintillate, scintillate, globule auriffic!
> Fain would I fathom thy nature specific.
> Loftily poised in the ether capacious,
> Strongly resembling a gem carbonaceous,
> Scintillate, scintillate, globule auriffic!
> Fain I would fathom thy nature specific.

Listen to a special arrangement of this famous tune.

EL BARCO CHIQUITO
(THE LITTLE SHIP)

Traditional

Can you describe with motions:
    the way the beats are grouped?

the way the melody moves?

Can you describe with line, shape, or color:
    the same or different **form** of the phrases?
    the way the rhythm of the melody will move
    in relation to the shortest sound?

G   D7

Ha - bí - a un   bar - co   chi - qui - ti - to,
Il   é - tait   un   pe - tit na - vi - re,
1. Oh, there was   once   a   lit - tle   ship,___

D7   G

ha - bí - a un   bar - co   chi - qui - ti - to,
il   é - tait   un   pe - tit na - vi - re,
oh, there was   once   a   lit - tle   ship,___

182

que no sa - bí - bí - bí - a na - ve - gar,
qui n'a - vait ja - ja - ja - mais na - vi - gué,
And it had ne - ne - nev- er made a trip,

que no sa bí - bí - bí - a na - ve - gar.
qui n'a - vait ja - ja - ja - mais na - vi - gue.
And it had ne - ne - ne - ver made a trip.

O - é, o - é._____ é._____
O - hé, o - hé._____ hé._____
O - ay, o - ay._____ boy._____

2. It sailed around through waters cold,
   Till no more foo-foo-food was in the hold.

3. And then the men the straws did deal
   To see just who-who-who would make their meal.

4. The shortest straw the youngest drew,
   So he was de-de-destined to be stew.

5. Meanwhile the boy climbed up the mast,
   Hoping a shi-shi-ship would soon come past.

6. But not a thing was there to see,
   And so he fear-fear-feared they'd soon eat he.

7. And, as he prayed, fish by the peck
   Suddenly la-la-landed on the deck.

8. They ate the fish with shouts of joy,
   And did not ea-ea-eat the cabin boy.

GO DOWN THE WISHIN' ROAD

Words and Music Arranged by Albert Stanton,
Jessie Cavanaugh, and Blake Alphonso Higgs

Calypso Folk Song

Perform these patterns.

Not syncopated

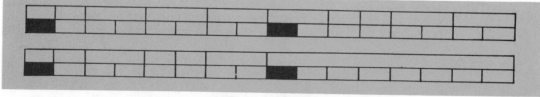

Syncopated

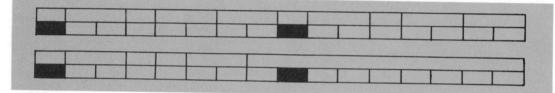

Can you describe **syncopation** with words?
Can you see places where syncopation will occur in this song?

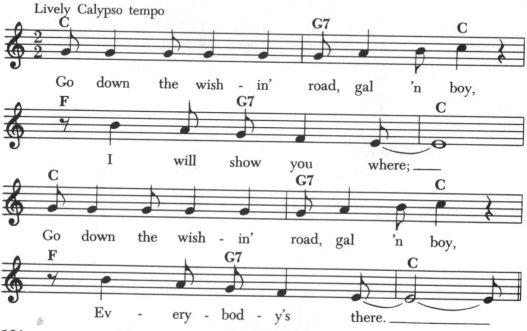

Lively Calypso tempo

Go down the wish - in' road, gal 'n boy,

I will show you where; ___

Go down the wish - in' road, gal 'n boy,

Ev - ery - bod - y's there. ___

184

Perform this percussion score.
Add it as an accompaniment to "Go Down the Wishin' Road."

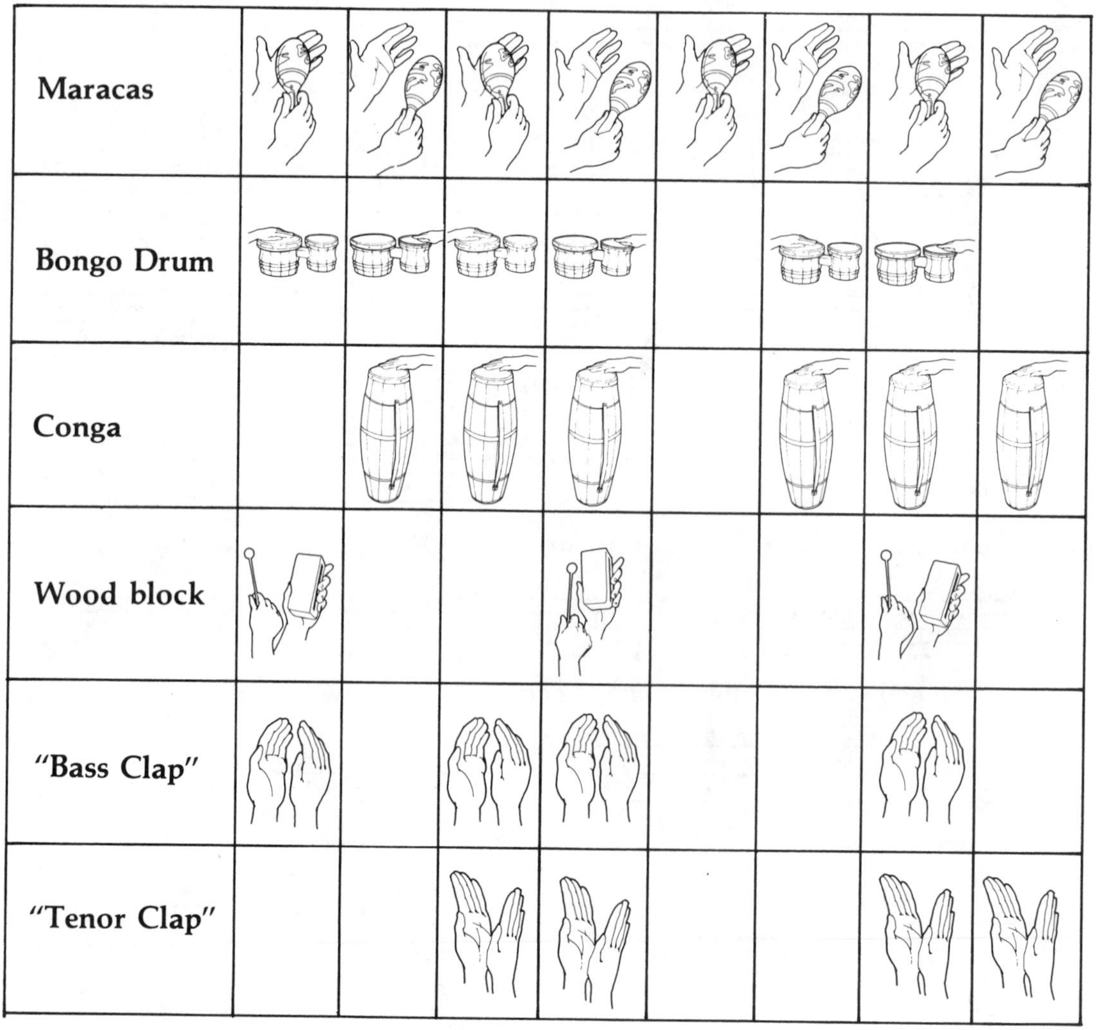

NOCTURNE
from *Divertissement*

by Jacques Ibert

Follow the leader . . .
move to the sounds
of whirring cymbals.

Listen to the music.

Move with your partner. Close
your eyes. Touch fingertips.
Follow the fingertips of your partner.

When will you move low? high?
Will your movements be smooth
and connected, or sharp and
disconnected?

187

THE MESSAGE OF SILENCE

Section A: All
I speak _____.
Can you hear?

Section B: Solos
I talk of Love,
I talk of Honor,
I talk of Need,
I talk of Hope,
I talk of Pride,
I talk of Respect,
I talk of Mankind.

Section A: All
I speak _____.
Can you hear?

I   speak

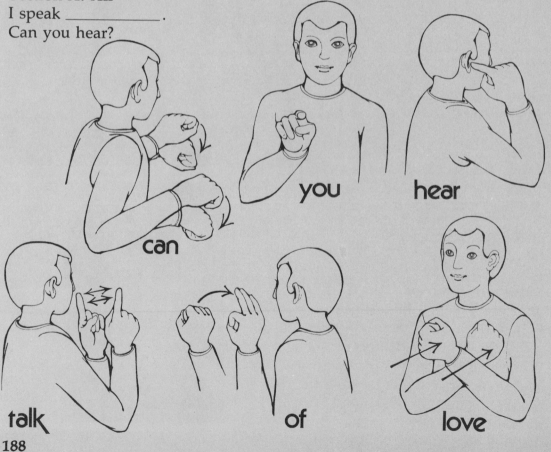

can   you   hear

talk   of   love

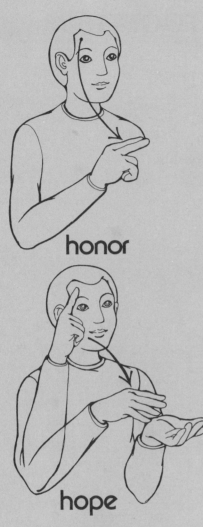

honor

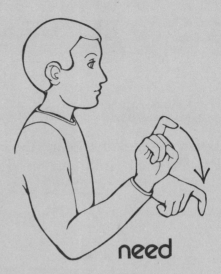

need

hope

pride

respect

mankind

LET US SING TOGETHER

Hand Signs Arranged
by Janet Cole

Adapted from a
Czech Folk Song

Learn the melody. Learn the hand signs.
Practice them until you can do them as you sing.

let   us   sing   together

Let us sing to-geth – er, Let us sing to-geth – er

One and all a joy – ous song. Let us sing to-

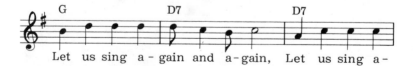

geth – er, One and all a joy – ous song.

Let us sing a-gain and a-gain, Let us sing a-

gain and a-gain, Let us sing a-gain and a-gain,

One and all a joy – ous song.

one

and

all .

a

happy

song

again

BRETHREN IN PEACE TOGETHER

Paraphrase of Psalm 133:1

Jewish Folk Song

This song and "Let Us Sing Together" (page 190) have the same key signature. One is based on a major scale; the other is based on a minor scale.

How can you decide which is major and which is minor? Study the notation for clues.

G Major	G		A	B	C		D		E		F#	G
E Minor	E		F#	G		A		B	C		D		E

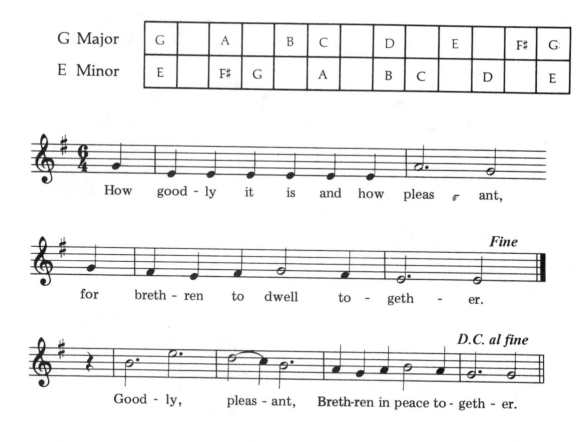

How good-ly it is and how pleas-ant,

for breth-ren to dwell to-geth-er. *Fine*

Good-ly, pleas-ant, Breth-ren in peace to-geth-er. *D.C. al fine*

THE SNAKE

Words and Music
by Marshall Barron

Play this accompaniment while singing the song.

Alto Metallophone

Sing in unison, then as a round.

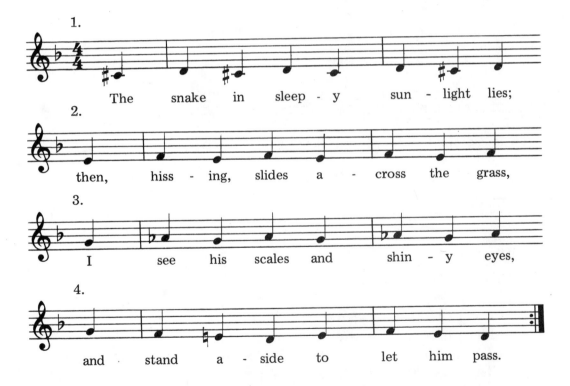

1. The snake in sleep - y sun - light lies;
2. then, hiss - ing, slides a - cross the grass,
3. I see his scales and shin - y eyes,
4. and stand a - side to let him pass.

Create an interlude. What instruments or vocal sounds could you use to describe the movement of the snake?

THE LOST LADY FOUND

English Folk Song

1. 'Twas down in a valley a fair maid did dwell,
She lived with her uncle, as all knew full well,
'Twas down in the valley where violets were gay,
Three gypsies betrayed her, and stole her away!

2. Long time she'd been missing and could not be found,
Her uncle, he searched the country around,
Till he came to her trustee, between hope and fear,
The trustee made answer "She has not been here."

3. The trustee spake up with a courage so bold,
"I fear she's been lost for the sake of her gold;
So we'll have life for life, sir," the trustee did say,
"We shall send you to prison, and there you shall stay."

4. There was a young squire that loved her so,
   Oft times to the school house together they did go;
   "I'm afraid she is murdered; so great is my fear,
   If I'd wings like a dove I would fly to my dear!"

5. He travelled through England, through France
         and through Spain,
   Till he ventured his life on the watery main;
   And he came to a house where he lodged for a night,
   And in that same house was his own heart's delight.

6. When she saw him, she knew him, and flew to his arms,
   She told him her grief while he gazed on her charms.
   "How came you to Dublin, my dearest, I pray?"
   "Three gypsies betrayed me, and stole me away."

7. "Your uncle's in England; in prison doth lie,
   And for your sweet sake is condemned for to die,"
   "Carry me to old England, my dearest," she cried;
   "One thousand I'll give you, and will be your bride."

8. When she came to old England, her uncle to see,
   The cart it was under the high gallows tree.
   "Oh, pardon! oh, pardon! oh, pardon! I crave!
   Don't you see I'm alive, your dear life to save?"

9. Then straight from the gallows they led him away,
   The bells they did ring, and the music did play;
   Every house in the valley with mirth did resound,
   As soon as they heard the lost lady was found.

ABALONE

Arranged by William S. Haynie

American Folk Song

1. In Mon - te - rey the peo - ple say, "We feed the laz - za - ro - ni
2. Oh, some folks boast of quail on toast be - cause they think it's ton - y,

On car - a - mels and cock - le - shells and hunks of ab - a - lo - ne."
But my tom - cat gets nice and fat on hunks of ab - a - lo - ne.

Refrain

Ab - a - lo - ne, _____ ab - a - lo - ne, _____

Ab - a - lo - ne, _____ ab - a -

_____ ab - a - lo - ne, _____ And hunks of ab - a -

lo - ne, _____ ab - a - lo - ne, And hunks of ab - a -

lo - ne, 'ba - lo - ne, 'ba - lo - ne.

lo - ne, 'ba - lo - ne, 'ba - lo - ne.

196

DESCRIBE A CHORD

Work in pairs.

    Follow the instructions on Guide Sheet "Describe a Chord."

    Discover the names of the pitches that belong to each chord.

    What **scale steps** are used to make up each chord?

Plan an accompaniment for "Old Farmer John."

Use any of these sounds:

    Bells   **Voices**   **Autoharp**   **Piano**

OLD FARMER JOHN

Canadian Folk Song

1. Old Farm - er ___ John from his work came home One
2. He sang as the cows came ___ run - ning by And
3. The old - est ___ cow in the farm - er's herd Tried

sum - mer ___ af - ter - noon, And sat him down in a
round him ___ formed a ring, For they nev - er heard old ___
hard to ___ join the song, But she could not strike the ___

ma - ple grove, And sang him - self a tune.
Farm - er John Be - fore at - tempt to sing.
mel - o - dy Though her voice was loud and strong.

197

NA LEI O HAWAII

English Words Adapted
from a text by Mary K. Pukui

Music by Samuel Kapu

Use the information you discovered when completing the
Guide Sheet, "Describe a Chord."
Build the **I, IV,** and **V7** chords in the **key of G.**
Decide which chords you will need to accompany this song.
You will need one for each box shown above the staff.

1. O fair-est Ha-wai-i, ___ fair le-i is-land, ___
2. O north-ern Kau-a-i, ___ green mo-ki-ha-na, ___
3. A le-i bring to me ___ of sand-y pu-pu, ___

Our gar-land is-land, we wear your red le-hu-a.
Fair mo-ki-ha-na grows high up-on your moun-tains.
The gleam-ing pearl-y shells of Ni-hi-a-u Is-land.

4. Kaulana Oahu your fine ilima,
   Your fine ilima with dainty fragrant blossoms.

5. On isle of Molokai on the candle nut tree,
   Grow silver kukui, leafy silver lei.

6. On little Lanai sweet Kaunaoa
   Sweet Kaunaoa is woven in your garland.

7. For you on Maui are lokelani,
   Are lokelani, red roses for your lei.

8. On peaceful shores, the shores of Kahoolawe,
   On Kahoolawe, come gather hinahina.

9. Ha'ina ia mai ana ka puana,
   Na lei o Hawaii e o mai.

10. Ha'ina hou ia mai ana ka puana,
    Hiiaka ia ka poli o Pele.

In which verse can you hear this descant played by the Hawaiian guitar?
Can someone sing it or play it on the metallophone?

MIGILDI MAGILDI

Words by Jack Dobbs

Welsh Folk Song
Arranged by Kurt Miller

This is a Welsh work song. It is based on the work rhythm of
the blacksmith and should be sung in a robust style with strong
accents and an **andante** tempo.
The words have no special meaning; they are just rhythmic
syllables imitating the sound of the hammer and anvil.

From the an - vil gay sparks glanc-ing,
When with-out the winds are blow-ing, } Mi-gil-di ma-gil-di hi now now,
Clang of ham-mer, blow of bel-lows,

Boldly

'Neath the black-smith's ham-mer danc-ing,
And in - side the fire is glow-ing, } Mi-gil-di ma-gil-di hi now now.
In the com - p'ny of good fel-lows,

Hi now ho now, Mi-gil-di ma-gil-di hi now now.

CREATE A WORK SONG

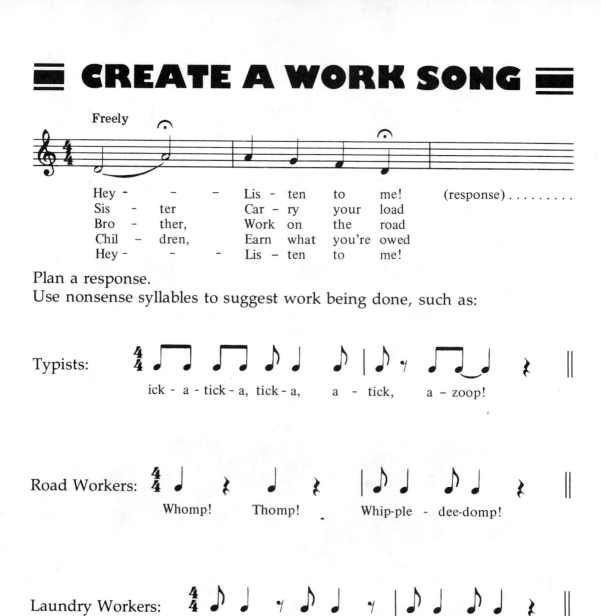

Freely

Hey - - - Lis - ten to me! (response)........
Sis - ter Car - ry your load
Bro - ther, Work on the road
Chil - dren, Earn what you're owed
Hey - - - Lis - ten to me!

Plan a response.
Use nonsense syllables to suggest work being done, such as:

Typists:
ick - a - tick - a, tick - a, a - tick, a - zoop!

Road Workers:
Whomp! Thomp! Whip-ple - dee-domp!

Laundry Workers:
shis - sha, wash - a, shis-sha sha wam

Sing your response using these pitches:

What other work sounds can you add?

202

The Match Game (1)

The Match Game: 1
Play "The Match Game."
Listen to some music.
Raise your hand as soon as you recognize the tune the composer used as the **theme** for this music.
If you recognize the theme, you should be able to pick the picture that describes the title.

a "lost lady"

As you listen to each composition more carefully, talk about the ways the composer took "old ideas" and made them "new."

203

LOST LADY FOUND
from *Lincolnshire Posy*

by Percy Grainger

Follow the chart as you listen to the composer's use of an ancient melody. Then add movements to describe the form.

THE MUSIC (Theme and Variations)	MOVEMENT
1. The theme is stated simply, in unison, by two clarinets.	Listen to, and feel, the underlying accent.
2. A chordal accompaniment is added by brass instruments.	**Group 1:** Move in this way: heel – toe – stamp, stamp, stamp
3. The lower brasses play a rhythmic accompaniment of broken chords.	**Group 1:** Repeat your ideas while a soloist adds an improvised movement.
4. The piccolo plays the melody, now very *legato*.	**Group 2:** Two members begin the movement—out, in, turn around. . . .
5. Other instruments join in playing the *legato* version of the melody.	**Group 2:** All members join the movement.

6. The French horn plays a countermelody.	**Group 2:** Continue, while a soloist improvises.

7. The accompaniment is again very rhythmic; the theme is in the low brasses. Then. . .	**Group 3:** Move this way:
	
	$\frac{3}{4}$ ♩ ♩ ♩ ♩ ♩ ♩
	   pat clap clap pat clap clap
	   knees
	
	♩ ♩ 𝄽 ♩ ♩ 𝄽 𝄽
	  step together step
	  sideways sideways

8. a trumpet is heard above the other brasses; suddenly a fanfare announces. . .	**Group 3:** Continue.
9. the big, majestic statement of the theme played by the full band and timpani.	**All Groups:** Repeat movements, this time reflecting the full, heavy sounds of the accompaniment.

Listen again to the other compositions you heard when playing ''The Match Game.'' Choose one, and prepare a chart to describe what you heard.

TINA SINGU

African Folk Song

Wat - sha, Wat - sha, Wat - sha, _____

la, la - la - la - la - la, la - la - la - la - la -

Wat - sha, _____ Wat - sha, _____

la, la - la - la - la - la la, la - la - la - la - la -

Wat - sha, Wat - sha, Wat - sha.

la, la - la - la - la - la - la.

Experiment with these rhythm patterns as you sing "Tina Singu."

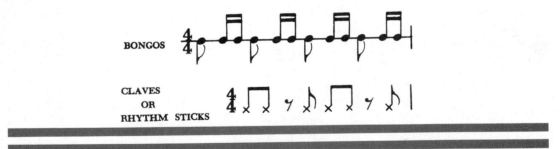

BONGOS

CLAVES
OR
RHYTHM STICKS

IF I HAD A HAMMER

Words and Music
by Lee Hays and Pete Seeger

This year you have learned music from many places and times.
Listen to the recording of this song.
From what time or place do you think the composers
got their ideas?

1. If I had a ham - mer, ___ I'd ham - mer in the
   bell, _____ I'd ring it in the
   song, _____ I'd sing it in the
   ham - mer, ___ And I've ___ got a

   morn - ing, ___ I'd ham - mer in the eve - ning, ___
   morn - ing, ___ I'd ring it in the eve - ning, ___
   morn - ing, ___ I'd sing it in the eve - ning, ___
   bell, _____ And I've ___ got a song, _____

   all o - ver this land; I'd ham - mer out
   all o - ver this land; I'd ring ___ out
   all o - ver this land; I'd sing ___ out
   all o - ver this land; It's the ham - mer of

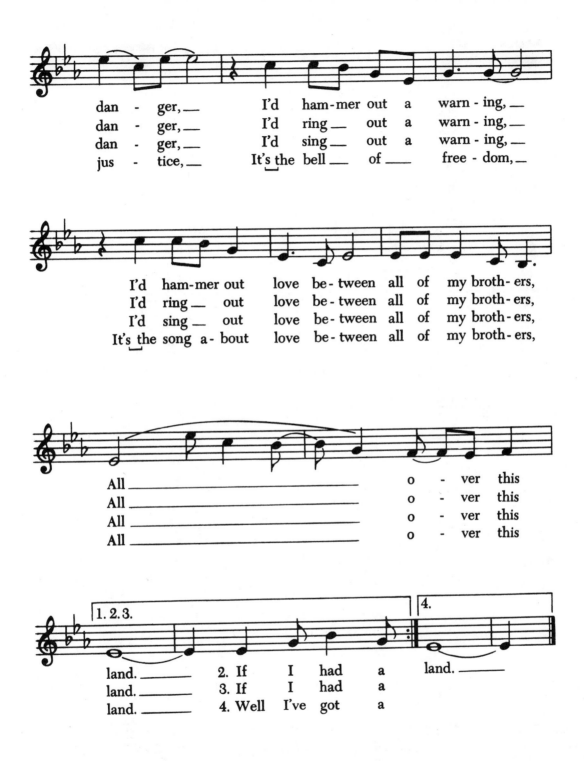

dan - ger, ___ I'd ham-mer out a warn - ing, ___
dan - ger, ___ I'd ring ___ out a warn - ing, ___
dan - ger, ___ I'd sing ___ out a warn - ing, ___
jus - tice, ___ It's the bell ___ of ___ free - dom, ___

I'd ham-mer out love be - tween all of my broth- ers,
I'd ring ___ out love be - tween all of my broth- ers,
I'd sing ___ out love be - tween all of my broth- ers,
It's the song a - bout love be - tween all of my broth- ers,

All _____ o - ver this
All _____ o - ver this
All _____ o - ver this
All _____ o - ver this

1. 2. 3.   4.

land. ___ 2. If I had a   land. ___
land. ___ 3. If I had a
land. ___ 4. Well I've got a

LONELINESS SONG

Navaho Indian Song
Adapted and Arranged
by Louis W. Ballard

What people first performed this music?
What do you think the words "adapted and arranged" mean?

GREEN RAINBOW

Indian Chant

Combine musical ideas and words to help express this Indian chant.

A green rainbow
  was moving toward me.

So, here I was,
  dancing under the rainbow.

Timpani

C G C G

Bass Xylophone

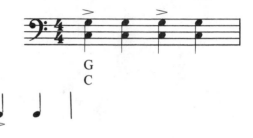

G
C

Hand Drum

I danced . . . and made the rain
  Wet the whole earth.

Danc-ing, danc-ing, un - der the rain-bow, green rain - bow.

≡ The Match Game (2) ≡

This is a harder match game.
These composers didn't use old tunes.
They wrote music that reflected the musical **heritage.**
Listen to each example.
Can you name the musical heritage the composer used as the
basis for the music?
Choose the picture you think describes the origin of the
musical ideas.

PIONEER DANCES

Introduction

by Peggy Stuart Coolidge

Thematic ideas

Most of the "Pioneer Dances" grow out of these thematic ideas.
Can you follow them through the composition?
What other instruments do you hear?
Make an up-to-date square dance to go with this modern
version of pioneer dances.
Form a square. Use some of these dance calls:

> Forward and back; do-si-do; honor your partner and
> your corner; swing your partner; swing the one across
> the hall; all promenade.

GOOD MORNING, BLUES

Words and Music
by Huddie Ledbetter

Can you describe the rhythm of the melody by:
- **showing** the relationship of each note to the shortest sound?
- **telling** the relationship of each note to the shortest sound?
- **performing** the rhythm in relation to the shortest sound?

1. Good morn-ing, blues; blues, how do you do?
2. Called yes-ter-day, here you come to-day.

Good morn-ing, blues; blues, how do you do?
Called yes-ter-day, here you come to-day.

I'm do-ing all right,— good morn-ing, how are you?
Your mouth's wide o-pen but you don't know what to say.

Can someone play this pattern on the piano or cello?

I-F   IV-Bb   V7-C7

You can also play this pattern on the autoharp.
Play the rhythm by making short, quick strokes on the lower strings.
Then play the chords and rhythm in this sequence, one pattern to a measure:

$\frac{4}{4}$ F | F | F | F | Bb | Bb | F | F | C | Bb | F | F ‖

OVER MY HEAD

Spiritual
Arranged by Buryl A. Red

O - ver my head _____

O - ver my

air. _____

I hear mu - sic in the air, in the air. _____ There

head I hear mu - sic in the air, in the air. _____

where. _____

must be a God some - where, some - where.

TWO WINGS

Refrain — Spiritual

Oh, Lord, I want two wings to veil my

Lord, I want to veil my

face; Oh, Lord, I want two wings to fly a-

face; Lord, I want to fly a-

way; Oh, Lord, I want two wings to veil my

way; Lord, I want to veil my

Fine
face, So the dev-il can't do me no harm.

Fine
face, So the dev-il can't do me no harm.

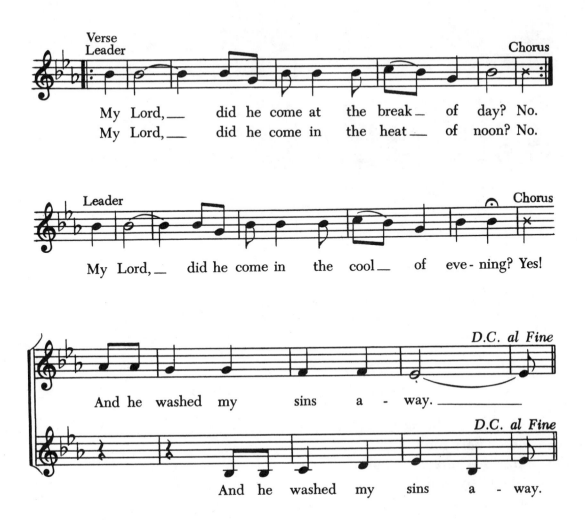

From its beginning, Afro-American music has been a blending
of many musical traditions. The spiritual, the work song, and
the blues combined musical traditions brought from Africa with
sounds of European music.

This blending of musical styles continues, as exhibited in modern
gospel music heard in churches and on television and
recordings.

CREATE YOUR OWN GOSPEL SONG

IN THE SWEET BY AND BY

Words by B. A.

Use the words of the poem.
Add a clapping accompaniment.
1. Soloist: Chant the rhythm you want to use.
2. Chorus: Echo the soloist, using "ch-ch" sounds to fill in the space between the end of one line and the beginning of the next.

Soloist	Chorus
There's a star in the sky,	_____
Lord, don't pass me by	_____
Cause that's where I'm comin',	_____
In the sweet by and by.	_____
By and by,	_____
By . . . and by . . .	_____
Yes, Lord, I'm coming,	_____
In the sweet by and by.	_____

3. Soloist: Make up a melody for the words. You may want to slide up and down and around to create a gospel sound.
4. Chorus: Decide on how you will echo. How many of the words will you use? Will you use parts of the sentence ("Yes . . . in the sky!"),

or

just words of agreement or concern ("Yes, yes!" "All right!" "Look out!" "By and by.")?
Sing your answer on the last pitch the soloist uses for each phrase.

PRODUCE A MUSICAL DRAMA

Musical dramas are staged in the same way that a dramatic play is produced.

In order to prepare a musical drama, you need a "stage" vocabulary.

Moving on the Stage
When the director wants to move players on the stage, directions are given such as, "Down stage, left," "Up stage, right."

Learn the way a stage is "blocked" so that you will understand where to go when the director tells you to move.

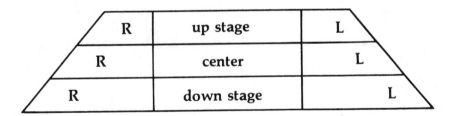

R	up stage	L
R	center	L
R	down stage	L

Choose one person to be the director.

Ten other people are the cast.

The director must give instructions, such as:
"John and Mary, down stage, left."
"Pierre and Tiboris, up, center stage."

How well does the cast follow instructions?

Setting the Scene

The director must know how to place people on the stage so that the view from the audience is effective.

Look at the following diagrams of people in a street scene. Which plan would be best for the audience to view?
Why?

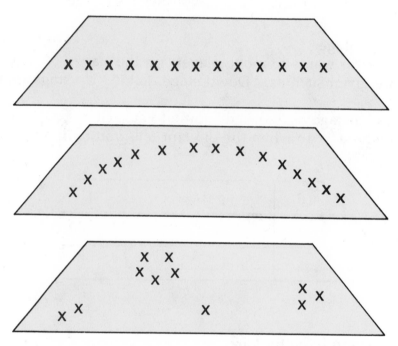

Focus

Often the main plot of a story is centered on one or two people, even though there are many others on stage. All performers must help the audience focus attention on the main characters.

Experiment with ideas for creating focus.
Set up "Street Scene."
Decide that the focus should be on Emile, the person who is down, center stage.

Here are some ways of drawing attention to Emile:
1. Each character looks only at members of his or her own group. There are no distracting movements or sounds.
2. One member of each group looks at Emile.
3. Everyone looks at Emile.
4. Everyone looks at Emile and leans slightly toward him.
5. Everyone leans slightly away from Emile.

Which focus has the most intensity, draws the most attention? Can you think of other ways of drawing attention to Emile?

Shifting Focus
As a drama unfolds, focus is shifted from one character to another.

An example: Remain in the Street Scene position.
Everyone is engaged in singing a soft conversation.
Emile begins to sing.
While Emile sings, one person in up stage center scratches the back of his (or her) leg with the shoe on the opposite foot.
What happens to the audience's attention?

Experiment with other ways of shifting focus from one individual in a group to another.
Now you're ready to try producing a musical play.

The Scene
A busy street

The Players
People on the street
(Who will you be? Why are you there? What will you do or say?)
The town's wealthy jeweler
Ragged Sam (or Samantha)—the one we can "see"
Ragged Sam's Conscience—the one who can
be seen only by Sam

The Plot
People are moving on the street, going about their business,
pausing to greet friends. The jeweler enters.
While walking down the street, he accidentally drops
a small box.
Ragged Sam is the only one who sees this happen.

First: Develop the dialogue as the plot unfolds.
"Talk" your parts.

Second: Repeat the performance. This time, "sing" the
scene.

Third: Evaluate the performance:
How well did the players move on the stage?
Do they need instructions or help with "blocking"?
Was the focus kept on the important character?
Did all players help shift focus at the right time?
How effective was the music?
Did the vocalists make changes in **dynamics, tempo,
articulation?**

Fourth: Try once more. Make changes based on your
evaluation of the second performance.

THE LONELY GOATHERD

from *The Sound of Music*

Words by Oscar Hammerstein 2nd

Music by Richard Rodgers

F **C7** **F** **C**

1. High on a hill was a lone - ly goat - herd, } lay - ee o-dl lay-ee o-dl
2. One lit - tle girl in a pale pink coat heard:

F **B♭** **F** **F** **C7** **F**

lay - ee - o. { Loud **was** the voice of the lone - ly goat - herd,
{ She yo-dled back to the lone - ly goat - herd,

Ho-di lay-ee, ____ Ho-di lay-ee, ____ Ho-di lay-ee, Ho-di lay-ee! ___

Accompaniment: Resonator bells or xylophone

Play **A** four times.
Play **B** once.
Play **A** four times.
Play **B** once.
Play **A** two times.
Play *Coda*.

Use small percussion instruments for special effects:

cowbell   wood blocks

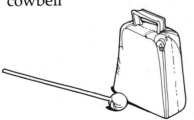
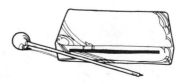

When this song was originally performed, marionettes were used to dramatize the story. Create your own marionettes. Use ideas as shown here, or design your own goatherd, little girl, mother, and herd of goats.

Stage this production.

Choose: 1. a musical director
2. composers and instrumental performers
3. a chorus
4. choreographers
5. stage hands
6. people to manipulate marionettes

Perform the drama that is told in the song.
Make your performance longer by creating a dance
for the herd of goats.
What kind of music will you play
to accompany the dance?
When will the goats dance?
Could the mother dance?
What kind of music will you create
for her dance?

THIS LAND IS YOUR LAND

Words and Music
by Woody Guthrie

1. As I was walk-ing that rib-bon of high-way,
2. I've roamed and ram-bled and I fol-lowed my foot-steps
3. When the sun comes shin-ing, and I ___ was stroll-ing

I saw a-bove me that end-less sky-way,
To the spar-kling sands of her dia-mond des-erts,
And the wheat-fields wav-ing and the dust clouds roll-ing,

I saw be-low me that gold-en val-ley,
And all a-round me a voice came sound-ing,
As the fog was lift-ing, a voice was chant-ing,

This land was made for you and me. ___

Refrain

This land is your land, this land is my land,

From Cal - i - for - nia to the New York is - land,

From the red - wood for - est to the Gulf Stream wa - ters;

This land was made for you and me. ____

The Three Witches

from *The Tragedy of Macbeth*

by William Shakespeare

Act Four, Scene 1

Scene: A cavern. In the middle, a boiling cauldron.

drum roll (thunder)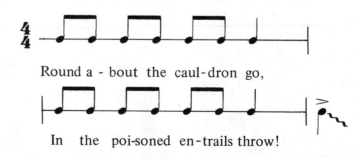

Enter the three witches.

Solo 1: (three awesome cat mews)

Solo 2: (four whines of a "hedge-pig." Use voices or slide whistles.)

First Witch: "Thrice the brinded cat hath mew'd."

Second Witch: "Thrice and once the hedge-pig whined."

Third Witch: Harpy cries, "'Tis time, 'tis time!"

Class: Make shuffling sounds in a steady beat. Continue throughout performance:

(Witches move around the cauldron to the shuffling sound, stirring as they go.)

Slowly

First Witch Chant:

Round a - bout the caul-dron go,

In the poi-soned en-trails throw!

Class Chant: (slowly, mysteriously)

p Dou – ble, dou – ble toil and trou – ble;

Fire burn and caul – dron bub – ble!

Dou – ble, dou – ble toil and trou – ble;

mp Bubble bubble, cauldron bubble, double trouble in a rubble.

f Fire burn and caul – dron bub – ble! *ff*

Phist! Whist! Fern churn, Bubbles in a cauldron BURN!

Second Witch Chant:

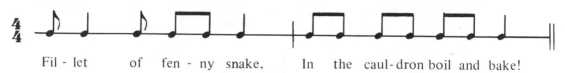

Fil - let   of fen - ny snake,   In   the caul - dron boil and bake!

Class Chant: (Repeat "Double, double, toil and . . .")

Third Witch Chant:

Scale of   dra - gon, tooth of wolf;   Witch - es' mum - my in   the gulf.

Class Chant: (Repeat "Double, double, toil and . . .")

All movement stops.

Second Witch: (slowly, as with wicked satisfaction)
"Cool it with the ash of wood,
Now the charm is firm and good!".

YOU'RE A GRAND OLD FLAG

Words and Music by George M. Cohan

You're a grand old flag, you're a high-fly-ing flag;

And for-ev-er in peace may you wave;____

You're the em-blem of the land I love,

The home of the free and the brave.____

Ev-ery heart beats true un-der red, white, and blue,

Where there's nev-er a boast or brag;____

But should auld ac-quaint-ance be for-got,

Keep your eye on the grand old flag.____

HARVEST

Translated by Judith Eisenstein

Hassidic Song

Joyously

Cut down the gol - den wheat, Bind it in stur - dy_ sheaves, oh! Pluck off the jui - cy grapes, Heap_ them in bas - kets_ high. Build a Su - kah co - vered with leaves, O - pen_ to the sky, for Now that our har - vest is in,

Slowly

Hal - le - lu - yah,_ Hal - le - lu - yah,_ Hal - le - lu - yah, we cry!

THANKSGIVING CANON

Traditional Canon

NOW THANK WE ALL OUR GOD

Words by Martin Rinckart
Translation by Catherine Winkworth

Melody by Johann Crüger

Listen to the recording of this well-known chorale. First you hear children sing it with an organ accompaniment written by Felix Mendelssohn. Then you hear Johann Sebastian Bach's arrangement which has been recorded with choir, two trumpets, and organ. The trumpets play interludes between the phrases which the choir sings.

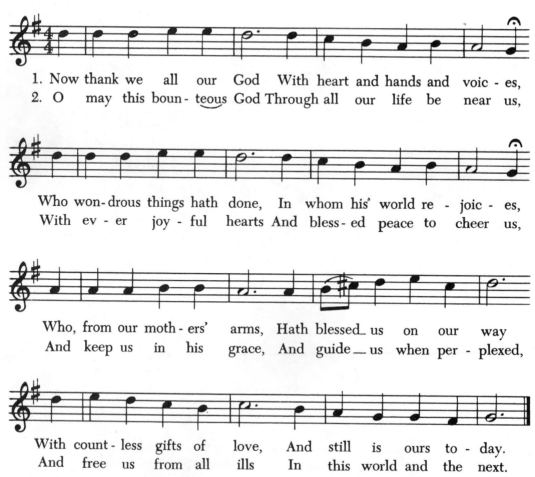

1. Now thank we all our God With heart and hands and voic - es,
2. O may this boun - teous God Through all our life be near us,

Who won-drous things hath done, In whom his' world re - joic - es,
With ev - er joy - ful hearts And bless - ed peace to cheer us,

Who, from our moth - ers' arms, Hath blessed us on our way
And keep us in his grace, And guide us when per - plexed,

With count - less gifts of love, And still is ours to - day.
And free us from all ills In this world and the next.

HERE WE COME A-WASSAILING

Old English Carol

1. Here we come a - was - sail - ing A - mong the leaves so green; __
2. We are not dai - ly beg - gars That beg from door to door; __
3. Good mas - ter and mis - tress, As you sit by the fire, __
4. God bless the mas - ter of this house, Like-wise the mis - tress, too, __

Here we come a - wan-d'ring, So fair __ to be seen.
But we are neigh-bors' chil-dren Whom you have seen be - fore.
Pray think of us poor chil-dren Who wan - der in the mire.
And all the lit - tle chil-dren That round the ta - ble go.

Refrain

Love and joy come to you, And to you glad Christ-mas

too; And God bless you and send __ you a hap - py New

Year, And God send you a hap - py New __ Year. __

239

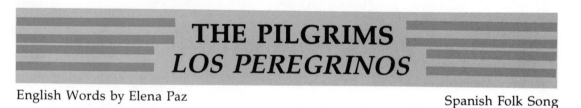

THE PILGRIMS
LOS PEREGRINOS

English Words by Elena Paz

Spanish Folk Song

Wearily

(*The pilgrims*) 1. From dis - tant lands so wea - ry,
(Los peregrinos) *1. De lar - ga jor - na - da*
(The Innkeepers) 2. Who, on this night so drear - y,

We've come up - on your door, ____
ren - di - dos lle - ga - mos,
Our com - fort dares dis - turb? ____

Night has ____ fall - en drear - y!
y a - sí lo im - plo - ra - mos
Here, by our blaze so cheer - y,

Wel - come us, we im - plore. ____
pa - ra des - can - sar. ____
Your pleas must go un - heard. ____

240

LA PIÑATA

Spanish Folk Song

Alla marcia

1. En las no - ches de po - sa - da, la pi -
2. Con tus o - ji - tos ven - da - dos y en las

ña - ta es lo me - jor; _____ Aun las ni - ñas re - mil
ma - nos un Bas - tón, _____ ¡la o - lla róm - pe - la a pe -

ga - das se a - ni - man con gran fer - vor:
da - zos! ¡No le ten - gas com - pa - sión!

Allegretto

Da - le da - le da - le, No pier - das el ti - no
Que si no le das _____ ¡de un pa - lo te e - pi - no!

mi - de la dis - tan - cia que hay en el ca - mi - no.
¡Por - que tie - nes au - ra, de pu - ro pe - pi - no!

HOW FAR TO BETHLEHEM?

Words Adapted from
G. K. Chesterton by Mary E. Caldwell

Music by Mary E. Caldwell

Flowing and rhythmic

1. How __ far to Beth-le-hem? Not ver-y far.

Shall we find the sta-ble-room lit by a star?

Can we see the lit-tle Child; __ is he __ with-in?

If we lift the wood-en latch, __ may we __ go in?

(Melody) Brighter

2. May we stroke the creat-ures there, __ ox-en and sheep?
May we watch like them and see __ Je-sus a-sleep?

Brighter

May we stroke them, ox-en and sheep?
May we watch __ Je-sus a-sleep?

If we touch his ti-ny hand, __ will he __ a-wake?

243

PAT-A-PAN

Words Adapted by Kurt Miller

French Carol
Arranged by Kurt Miller

Pat - a - pat- a - pan, Tu - re - lu - re - ley, Fife and drum to - geth-er play on this joy - ous hol - i - day.

1. Bil - lie, bring your new red drum; Rob-bie, get your
2. There is mus - ic in the air, you can hear it

1. Bil - lie
2. Mus - ic

SABBATH QUEEN

Words by Chaim N. Bialik
Translated by A. Irma Cohen

Music by P. Minkowsky
Arranged by Harry Coopersmith

The sun on the tree tops no long-er is seen, Come
Ha-cha-moh mey-rosh ho-ee lo-nos nis-tal-koh, Bo-

The sun on the tree tops no long - er, Come
Ha-cha-moh mey-rosh ho-ee lo - nos, Bo-

gath-er to wel-come the Sab-bath our Queen___, Be-
u v'-ney-tsey lik-ras Sha-bos ha-mal-koh, Hi-

gath-er to wel-come the Sab-bath our Queen___.
u v'-ney-tsey lik-ras Sha-bos ha-mal-koh.

hold her de-scend-ing, the ho - ly the blest With
ney hee yo-re-des hak'-do-shoh ha-b'ru-cho, V'-

With
V'-

THE STAR-SPANGLED BANNER

Words by Francis Scott Key

Music by John Stafford Smith

1. Oh, — say, can you see by the dawn's ear - ly light,
2. On the shore, dim - ly seen thro' the mists of the deep,
3. Oh, — thus be it ev-er when — free men shall stand

What so proud - ly we hailed at the twi-light's last gleam-ing?
Where the foe's haugh-ty host in dread si - lence re - pos - es,
Be - tween their loved homes and the war's des - o - la - tion!

Whose broad stripes and bright stars, through the per - il - ous fight,
What is that which the breeze, o'er the tow - er - ing steep,
Blest with vic - t'ry and peace, may the heav'n-res - cued land

O'er the ram - parts we watched were so gal - lant - ly stream-ing?
As it fit - ful - ly blows, half con - ceals, half dis - clos - es?
Praise the Pow'r that hath made and pre - served us a na - tion.

And the rock - ets' red glare, the bombs burst - ing in air,
Now it catch - es the gleam of the morn - ing's first beam,
Then — con - quer we must, for our cause it is just,

CLASSIFIED INDEX

ALPHABETICAL INDEX